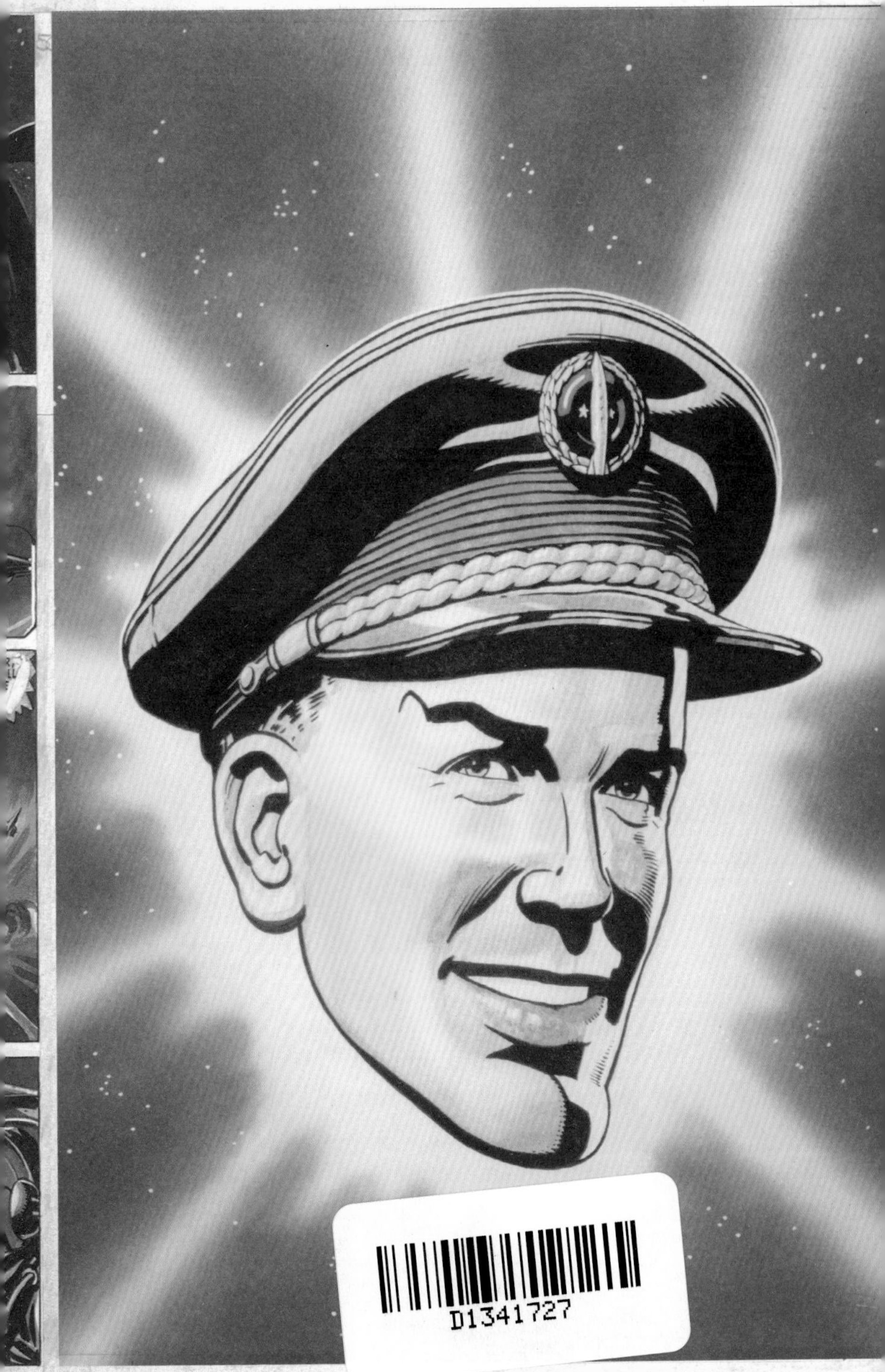

DAN DARE

Pilot of the Future

Also by Daniel Tatarsky

Flick to Kick: An Illustrated History of Subbuteo

(Editor)
Eagle Annual: Best of the 1950s Comic
Eagle Annual: Best of the 1960s Comic
The Eagle Annual of the Cutaways
Eagle Diary 2011

DAN DARE

Pilot of the Future

A BIOGRAPHY

DANIEL TATARSKY

Copyright © Colin Frewin and Associates 2010

The right of Colin Frewin and Associates to be identified as
the author of this work has been asserted by him in accordance with the
Copyright, Designs and Patents Act 1988.

This edition first published in Great Britain in 2010 by
Orion Books
an imprint of the Orion Publishing Group Ltd
Orion House, 5 Upper St Martin's Lane,
London WC2H 9EA
An Hachette UK Company

1 3 5 7 9 10 8 6 4 2

A CIP catalogue record for this book is available
from the British Library.

ISBN: 978 0 7528 8896 5

Printed and bound in Great Britain by CPI Mackays, chatham ME5 8TD

The Orion Publishing Group's policy is to use papers that are natural,
renewable and recyclable and made from wood grown in sustainable forests.
The logging and manufacturing processes are expected to conform to the
environmental regulations of the country of origin.

Every effort has been made to fulfil requirements with regard to
reproducing copyright material. The author and publisher will be glad to
rectify any omissions at the earliest opportunity.

www.orionbooks.co.uk

CONTENTS

AUTHOR'S NOTE

This book relies heavily on interviews, some of which were undertaken by me and a couple by other people.

Starting with the latter, I have to give credit and thanks to Alan Vince and Penny Sparke for the their interviews with Frank Hampson. Alan is a lifelong fan of the *Eagle* and Dan Dare and wanted to meet Frank for many years. After exchanging numerous letters the two finally met in January 1974 and Alan recorded their conversation on reel-to-reel tape. He transcribed the tape, and he and Frank revised and updated the text in 1976. Alan was kind enough to send me the typed manuscript of this conversation.

Penny Sparke gained a PhD in Design History at Sussex University in 1975, and went on to teach the subject. In 1978 she conducted a half-hour interview with Frank for Sussex University, which was recorded on VHS. I have transcribed Frank's answers for use herein.

I am responsible for the other interviews. The people I had the pleasure of meeting and chatting to in person were: Greta Tomlinson (who baked me a lovely cake), Peter Hampson, Adrian Perkins and Terry Jones (he kindly paid for the beer).

Other interviews were conducted by phone, email and old fashioned mail, with Margaret Jackson (Frank Hampson's sister), Don Harley, Bruce Cornwell, Alan Vince, Sir Tim Rice, David Lewis Gedge, Paul Cornell,

Bryan Talbot and Martin Bower.

In researching this book I found nothing but eager and helpful people wherever I turned and I would like to thank them all: Donald Brown (Weeley), Elizabeth Boardman (Brasenose), Christopher Tudor (Brasenose), Adrian Perkins, Denis Steeper, Will Grenham (*Eagle Times*), Jen Booth (Gen Sec Rossallian Club), Lemn Sissay, Paul Cornell, Sir Tim Rice, Diane O'Bannon, Martin Bower, John Freeman, Rod Barzilay (www.spaceshipaway.org. uk), Don Harley, Joan Porter, Greta Tomlinson, Bruce Cornwell, Roger Dobson, Gerald Scarfe, Nev Fountain, Howard Corn, Andrew Atherstone (Wycliffe Hall), Pete Crowther, Alastair Crompton, Kate Owens (Cartoon Museum), David Britton, Al Notton (www.comicsuk. co.uk), Roger Coombes, Bryan Talbot, James Robertson, Paul Bagshaw, Norman Wright, Adam Brockbank, David Lewis Gedge, David Scripps, Eryl Humphrey Jones, Sally Barker (Morris) . . . I hope I have named them all here but if I have missed anyone off I hope you'll forgive me.

I would also like to acknowledge the contribution of Lisa Parsley and Colin Frewin at the Dan Dare Corporation, their agent Gordon Wise and also Shaheeda Sabir from Curtis Brown.

I would also like to thank Ian Preece at Orion for sticking with Dan and myself through thick and thin and Vicki Harris for making sure this all makes sense. Any places where it doesn't are because I wouldn't listen to her sage advice.

Finally I'd like to thank Katie Cowan who makes everything and anything seem possible.

PERMISSIONS AND CREDITS

Dean Close School Archives Department, especially Charles Witney

Photo of Marcus Morris and wife: the Principal and Fellows of Brasenose College, Oxford

Quote from *The Man Who Drew Tomorrow*: courtesy of Alastair Crompton

Second Dummy: image courtesy of The Cartoon Museum

First Dummy: images courtesy of Sally Barker (Morris), Jan Hallwood and Lutterwoth Press.

Eagle Club Memorabilia Images: Howard Smith

Daily Mirror Extract: courtesy of the *Daily Mirror*

Kevin Slocombe, CWU: Cartoons from *The Post*.

Quotes from *Before I Die Again*, Chad Varah: courtesy of Constable Robinson

Calvert Tooth Powder Album: courtesy of John Liffen, Curator, Science Museum

Original photography by Giuliana Cassaroti

INTRODUCTION

by Terry Jones

On Friday the 14th April 1950 my elder brother disappeared on his bicycle for the shops and arrived back with a comic. My mother had a fit and wanted to throw the object out immediately. What would my father say when he discovered that one of his children had bought a *comic*?

Comics were forbidden items in our house. Probably they were forbidden in many households of the period. There was a feeling prevalent in the late 1940s and early 1950s that comic books were a Really Bad Thing. Schoolteachers, clergymen and others combined to advise parents that comics made children illiterate and were to blame for a lot of juvenile delinquency. I had heard some of the debates about this on the radio. Juvenile delinquency had nothing to do, of course, with the fact that the world had just been embroiled in seven years of warfare, with people being killed and tortured for real. No, it was down to the importing of horror comics from America.

I even remember, at school, glimpsing a copy of *Tales from the Crypt* in which someone was lowered into what looked like a swimming bath full of acid, and came out as a skeleton. I called to mind the warnings about how seeing such things could lead to depravity, and worried for weeks about having caught that glimpse. Would it trigger in me an impulse to dunk people in sulphuric acid or do something desperate to alter my psyche?

My brother, however, explained to my mum that this comic, the *Eagle*, was all right because it was edited by a *clergyman*. My mother wavered. Then she noted that it was published by the respectable publishing house The Hulton Press, responsible for such uncontroversial publications as *Picture Post* and *The Farmers Weekly*. Eventually she decided to hide the comic in a kitchen drawer, so that when my father came home she could prepare the ground, and thereby hopefully assuage his wrath.

As it turned out my father gravely examined the offending article and, after perusing it for some time, pronounced it acceptable and formally admitted it into the household.

We were free to enjoy the *Eagle* with clear consciences. It was officially endorsed by our parents (although they, of course, never read it – as far as we knew), and it was even delivered along with the newspaper every Friday. What bliss.

But for me the *Eagle* was *Dan Dare – Pilot of the Future*. I was blown away by Frank Hampson's flights of fantasy: the wonderful world of 1995, where a world government operated for the benefit of all, in shining cities of glass roofs and beautiful gardens, but where there was that familiar problem: a lack of food. But most of all it was the *other* worlds that seized my imagination. That wonderful panorama of the surface of Venus, in issue No. 9, filled with perfectly realized vegetation and animals that I'd never seen before or dreamed of – and yet all under-cut by Digby's laconic commentary: 'I don't see any bus stops round here or snack bars . . .'

The combination of fantasy and humour, for me, was irresistible. I was hooked.

What other comic book could leave you on a hook of Digby saying: 'Funny how you get the idea you're being watched' and then follow that with three frames in a row of strange animals, followed by a fourth, of an alien watching from the undergrowth? It was pure genius.

In *Dan Dare – Pilot of the Future, the Biography* Daniel Tatarsky celebrates, with a shrewd critical judgement, the achievement of Frank Hampson and his team, while at the same time placing the stories in the context of the 1950s. In so doing he presents a lot of history that I hadn't realized even though I lived through those years. For example he points out that bread was only rationed *after* the Second World War, and that the premise of the whole story – the quest for an alternative food supply for Earth – was extremely relevant in the days of shortages and rationing.

At the same time he makes many surprising behind-the-scenes revelations: such as that, in the original dummy of the *Eagle*, Dan Dare was actually a Space Fleet Chaplain, complete with black shirt and dog collar – echoing the *Eagle*'s founder and editor, Marcus Morris, who had of course been an RAF chaplain during the Second World War.

This book is an invaluable bringing together of the many strands that go to make Dan Dare such a rare and wonderful story. I am sure it will delight all Dan Dare fans and perhaps persuade those who are not familiar with him to turn over these much-loved pages.

Terry Jones, August 2010

PREFACE

During his interview with Penny Sparke in 1978, Frank Hampson, who, with the Reverend Marcus Morris, had jointly created the *Eagle*, suggests that it is difficult to understand the impact the magazine made when it was launched on the 14th April 1950. Even then, just twenty-eight years after the event, the world had moved on and the amazing colour, futuristic storylines and quality printing were commonplace. So, looking back now, sixty years after it first hit the streets, it is even harder to appreciate how the *Eagle* and, more specifically, its headline star Dan Dare, totally changed the landscape of the comic-reading world.

When the *Eagle* was launched, Frank Hampson had never worked on a boys' magazine, no one in the industry referred to these productions as comics, and Marcus Morris was still being paid to be a vicar. The publication they created used a state of the art printing process, photogravure, which was unheard of for a boys' comic. But it was the content that really made the difference, and it is Dan Dare that people still remember today.

Dan Dare was the chief pilot for the Interplanet Space Fleet and his adventures took place in a future beautifully imagined by Hampson and his studio of artists. With his sidekick Digby, and the rest of the crew, Sir Hubert Guest, Professor Peabody, Hank Hogan and

Pierre Lafayette, Dan made his mark across the universe. In their first adventure they went to Venus to find food for a starving Earth, and from that moment on the Pilot of the Future was a hero in his fictional world at the end of the twentieth century as much as he was for the readers in the middle of that century.

This biography explains how the *Eagle* was created, discusses the important people in its history and also looks at the adventures of Dan Dare, which were chronicled in its pages over two decades, during which time the country changed beyond recognition. These pages may act as a reminder of something you read in your youth, or are possibly a first taste of the thrills and spills of space travel 1950s style. Either way, Dan Dare is out there, watching and waiting to save us all if the need arises. He was created in a distant past but he will always be The Pilot of the Future.

DAN DARE
Pilot of the Future

CHAPTER ONE

The Birth of *Eagle*

Success has many fathers (*Count Caleazzo Ciano*)

IN NATURE, every animal has two parents. In most cases this is one male and one female. Dan Dare, who we know was special in many ways, was also special in having two fathers: Frank Hampson and Marcus Morris. This pairing may seem a match made in heaven – but they were from very different backgrounds and, while opposites are supposed to attract, they may not necessarily stay together for ever.

Throughout history there have always been partnerships that together are greater than they are alone. Would Laurel have been so funny without the straight-laced uptightness of Hardy? Would Lennon and McCartney have reached such amazing heights without their underlying creative tensions? (Frog Chorus, anyone?) And would Harold Larwood have destroyed the Aussies in the Bodyline Series without the workhorse back-up of his great friend Bill Voce?

It is fair to argue, in all three cases, that they never again hit the heights that they had reached during their time together. So it was with Hampson and Morris.

Morris went on to a very successful career in publishing, but whenever his name is mentioned now it is in relation to the *Eagle*, almost as though his work at the National Magazine Company never happened. In Frank Hampson's case the evidence is even clearer. He put everything he had into 'Dan Dare', and while he never lost the technical drawing skills after he walked out of the *Eagle* offices for the last time, he never came close to matching the work he did in creating, developing and maintaining his favourite fictional son.

For Hampson, 'Dan Dare' was very much like the greatest race an athlete has ever run. He left absolutely everything on the track. For readers and comic-strip aficionados this leaves a treasure of insurmountable value, but Frank himself would never be the same again. Greta Tomlinson, one of the other artists from the strip, remembers visiting him after he had left the *Eagle*. 'I couldn't believe it, how insecure he was, he was a completely different person. He'd completely lost confidence. He said, "I'll never draw again, Greta."' In fact, for long spells in the years between his departure and his death almost twenty-five years later he could not even bring himself to put pencil to paper.

At the first meeting of Marcus Morris and Frank Hampson, sparks didn't fly, the earth did not shake (but apart from in films, and comics maybe, that never actually happens). It was a simple job offer from a vicar running a parish magazine to a local artist with a growing reputation.

There seem to be two opposing versions of what life was like in Britain after the war. In one, everyone was so joyously delighted to be alive that everything and anything seemed possible. In the other, the country was suffering from shortages of basic foodstuffs, major cities were still scarred by bombing raids and life was anything but sweet. As usual the truth lies somewhere in between, and for ambitious, hard-working folk the opportunities were there if you searched deeply enough. Our lives are affected by the people we meet, but we only meet them because of what we have done up to the point of that meeting.

On 25 April 1915 Walter Edmund Harston Morris and his wife Edith, née Nield, welcomed their second child, John Marcus Harston Morris, into the world. All the children in the family were given the third name of Harston. Like his father before him Walter was a vicar, and by now was working in his second appointment at the Emmanuel Church in Preston. They already had a daughter, Edith Mary, and following Marcus would have two more sons, Walter Edward and Peter David. Tragically David died, aged just five, following an allegedly botched appendix operation. Edward, or Teddy as the family knew him, went on to become a rubber planter.

Not long after Marcus's birth the family moved to Southport, where Walter had been appointed to All Saints. Following on from a brief nine-month sojourn in the sleepy village of Balderstone, this posting lasted a great deal longer and saw the family stay for thirty-eight years.

Marcus's serious education began at the public school Dean Close in Cheltenham, when he entered Tower

House at the beginning of the Lent term of 1929. The school's other most famous old boys are the artist Francis Bacon and Brian Jones of the Rolling Stones. Morris attended shortly after the former and well before the latter, at a time when the school was under the guidance of only its second headmaster since opening in 1886. Loyalty and continuity therefore were clearly an important part of the establishment and these qualities were impressed on its pupils.

The new head, Percy Bolton, introduced the house system into the school, and Morris's housemaster was C. A. P. Tuckwell, who directed many of the school plays, helping build the school's theatre along the way (and, quite rightly, having it named after him). It was no surprise therefore that Marcus became heavily involved with the stage and, among other roles, played Viola in *Twelfth Night*, with 'taste and talent' according to E. M. Phair's *History of the Tuckwell Theatre 1926–98*.

He did not confine himself purely to artistic endeavours. As was to be seen throughout his life, his interests and energies were applied across the whole spectrum of what the school had to offer. In fact, when looking at the list of his activities, it seems hard to believe that he had time for any study. He was a school prefect and a platoon sergeant in the Officer Training Corps. He gained school colours in hockey, athletics and cross-country running, of which team he was captain in 1933 and 1934.

When not in a uniform of one sort or another he played the cello and conducted his house's entry to the house music competition in 1934. Just reading the list makes one breathless, but did this fulfil him or give him cause to slow down? Of course not. He was in his mid-teens and his energy had no limits. He was also a school librarian, won the Greek Testament Prize in 1933 and was even briefly assistant secretary of the Photographic Society. Whoever the secretary was at the time must have feared for his job, such was the force of nature called Morris.

So it seems there was little that the young Marcus did not try, and maybe this gives the impression of a jack of all trades. But it must be this scattergun nature of his attention that enabled him to produce a comic that appealed across the board. He wasn't just a sportsman, didn't restrict himself to the arts or get buried in science. He seems to have been genuinely fascinated by it all. Today we might say he had a short attention span or was in need of therapy, but it seems quite obvious from what he went on to achieve that he was driven and inquisitive to an unusually high degree.

But could he focus? Did he have some core beliefs that drove him on? Perhaps his participation in a debate at a meeting of the Literary Society shows some of the first signs of what his future held. The *Decanian*, the school magazine, records him opposing the motion that 'This House disapproves the system of universal education'. He opened his argument thus: 'It is the duty of every state to educate its people,' and went on to say that he believed that everyone must be a thinking being, not merely doing a job mechanically. Education, he contin-ued, brings that situation about and it would improve the general standard of living and enable people to develop their own ideals and philosophy. He ended by stating that 'to educate the populous [*sic*] merely to earn a living was an insult to civilisation'. The motion was thus defeated.

'To educate the populace merely to earn a living is an insult to civilisation.' Here was a young man, just starting out in life, who must have felt his life, and living, was laid out for him. His father and his father's father had both been vicars. This was what was planned for him, and he could see that there was more to life than just earning a wage, more to be done than merely following in the footsteps of those who had gone before. He didn't know at the time what this might be, but he knew that education and knowledge were more than just means to pay the bills. They were an end in themselves, an important end, and one that less than two decades later he would pour into his creation.

In between sport, arts and square-bashing Marcus did well enough in the classroom at Dean Close to gain entry into the all-male Brasenose College, Oxford. He matriculated, i.e. underwent the formal ceremony of admittance as a member of the university, in 1934 with a Colquitt Exhibition. This scholarship was one of three founded specifically for the benefit of undergraduates studying for holy orders by the Misses Elizabeth, Lucy and Susannah Colquitt in 1842 in memory of their brother Scrope Milner Colquitt, who died five months after graduating from Brasenose in 1825. This, along with his heritage, tied him in further to a career in the Church. The scholarship enabled him to attend university, but he was mixing in a rarefied society whose bank balances were somewhat in advance of his. This period of high living set a trend for the years to come, when his income would not always match his outgoings.

In these years just prior to the Second World War life at Oxford offered a last glimpse of freedom and extravagance. Even though knowledge of the growth of the National Socialists in Germany was common among the well-travelled élite at the university, there was not, until the later 1930s, a sense of what the party would become and how it would affect the world. Marcus even saw it at close quarters during a canoeing trip down the Danube in 1937. In spite of this first-hand knowledge, the students attending the numerous dinners and parties and balls did not realise that they were at the end of an era. Like most people in their late teens and early twenties, they felt they would live for ever and had no intention of depriving themselves.

One contemporary at Brasenose was John Profumo, who would later find infamy due to his affair with Christine Keeler, which led to his resignation from the government and perhaps contributed to the Conservatives' defeat in the general election of 1964. The present Prime Minister, David Cameron, also attended Brasenose, as did the founder of the *Picture Post*, Edward George Warris Hulton. Remember that name.

While Marcus had thrown himself into everything at Dean Close, the opposite appears to have been the case at Brasenose. He confessed to feeling that he never truly felt part of the college. Maybe it was due to his financial shortcomings, or perhaps a lack of self-confidence, but either way Marcus felt that he didn't participate fully in the academic or sporting sides of life at Brasenose. This can often happen at university. Having been a big fish in a small pond at Dean Close, suddenly he was swimming with undergraduates who had all been big fish back home, and not everyone could be the leader. He did play hockey for the college though, as well as being a member of the athletics team, and on 14 October 1937 he was awarded his BA, a second-class degree in Classics.

As far back as he could remember his family had been in the Church; he had been able to attend Brasenose thanks to an ecclesiastical grant; and so it was inevitable that his next step would continue in that direction – although he did have doubts during his time at Brasenose. In the end his religious conviction held out: he felt that when all was said and done Christian philosophy made sense to him. He thus completed his final preparations for such a life by staying in Oxford and moving slightly north, where he was enrolled at the theological college Wycliffe Hall. In 1939 he achieved a second-class degree in Theology.

It was while at Oxford that Marcus met and fell heavily in love with Rita Foyle, a model from London. As was to be his modus operandi, Marcus did not let the grass grow under his feet, and it was only a few months after meeting her in the summer of 1938 that Rita was introduced to his parents and their engagement was announced.

With war having recently been declared, Marcus was ordained deacon in Liverpool Cathedral in late September 1939. He only had to travel seven miles to his first parish and church, St Bartholomew's in Roby, on the outskirts of Liverpool. The vicar at the time, Charles Richard Jarvis, was quite early into a long incumbency that would last until 1970, and Marcus was installed as his junior curate. One of Marcus's duties was to recruit new parishioners. The favoured method was going from door to door with the word of Christ. Marcus never took to this.

Roby was undergoing many changes, which would be accelerated by the war. Up until the 1930s it could still have been thought a rural area, occupied by a farming community, but gradually the city was encroaching and housing schemes led to many hundreds of new houses being built.

In spite, or maybe because, of the war raging just the other side of the Channel, Marcus was determined to marry Rita as soon as possible. He approached the Bishop of Liverpool for permission, but the rules of the diocese meant that he would not be allowed to marry before completing two years as a curate. Marcus would not give up, though, and kept badgering away until Bishop David gave way – but only on the condition that Marcus found another curacy.

After various possibilities had come and gone, Canon Robert Aubrey Aitken at St Nicholas' Church in Great Yarmouth offered Marcus a job. Delighted that the obstacle in the way of his desire for marriage had now gone, Marcus arranged to meet Rita for a trip to Great Yarmouth to look for somewhere for them both to live. They were due to meet at Euston Station for the journey but not only did Rita arrive late, she came bearing bad tidings. Her heart had been taken by another, a naval officer, and the engagement was therefore off.

With the breaking-off of his wedding plans Marcus would have preferred to stay in Roby, near to his family and friends, but had already committed to the job in

Great Yarmouth and so had to move. As it turned out his absence was quite short.

The north-west, and specifically Liverpool, was a major target for German bombing during the war. In fact, it was the most heavily targeted area outside of London, and not long after Marcus's move to the east coast, this bombardment would have an indirect effect on his future. In mid-April 1941 he received an urgent telegram from home informing him that his parents had been bombed out, and although they were safe his mother asked if he would come home. Edith had not been injured but Walter was in hospital. Southport was in fact a place where children from Liverpool were sent to avoid the danger of regular bombings on the big industrial city and important port. Unfortunately, it was also on the route back for those very same German planes, and occasionally they would drop their unused ordnance on the coastal town. It was this accident of geography that put Morris's parents on the flight path and thus redirected his life.

It was on this trip that much of Marcus's future would be set, and his broken heart repaired. On arriving in Southport his fears of the worst were allayed, and once he had made sure his father was not in grave danger he decided to make the most of his trip back home and thus met up with an old friend, Joe Crossley.

He and Crossley, a journalist on the *Southport Guardian*, went to the Little Theatre. Under normal circumstances this was the home of the Southport Dramatic Club, and had been since 1937. (It is still running today.) During the war, though, the club only put on three plays, but the theatre was sub-let to the Sheffield

Repertory Company, which had, ironically given the circumstances of Marcus's visit, itself been stopped from
putting shows on in its own theatre due to the danger of
bombings. Sheffield's loss was Southport's, and on this
night Marcus Morris's, gain. The show he and Joe went
to see was *Marigold*, a Scottish romantic comedy which
a couple of years previously had been released as a film.
On stage that night the eponymous heroine, Marigold
Sellar, was being played by Jessica Dunning.

Crossley took Morris backstage after the performance
and introduced him to Jessica. In wartime, emotions
are heightened and time is compressed. According to all
sources it was love at first sight. If Marcus had moved
quickly to secure his engagement to Rita, it was with even
more amazing alacrity that within ten days of meeting
Jessica he had proposed and been accepted.

It was maybe because he had let the girl get away on
the previous occasion that Marcus made sure there was
no escape this time and, less than a month after meeting,
they were married on 13 May 1941 at All Saints Church,
Southport.

Marcus was eager to do his bit for the war effort in
the best way he could and therefore decided to take his
ministry to the armed services. Towards the end of July
1941 he got his wish and received news that he was to be
posted to RAF Bircham Newton, Kings Lynn, not far
from Great Yarmouth. Someone, somewhere, obviously
had a sense of humour. He was to begin work in early
August and was given the rank of Squadron Leader,
Chaplain's Branch, Royal Air Force Volunteer Reserve.
Jessica was still appearing on stage in Southport and so

once again Marcus made the journey to the east coast alone, although they kept in touch regularly by letter.

He was only to stay for a few weeks, until mid-August 1941, before a reorganisation had him posted to RAF Cosford, near Wolverhampton. It was at Cosford that Marcus first tried his hand at taking the Church to the people. In effect, this meant drinking and playing trad- itional pub games in the officers' mess. No one there appeared to mind his presence, but the Bishop of Lich- field received a complaint, maybe from someone who lost at shove-ha'penny, and Marcus was admonished.

His time at Cosford was a little longer-lived, but by March of the next year he was on his way again, this time to RAF Benson, about fifteen miles south-east of Oxford. As the only Church of England chaplain at the base, Marcus was optimistic that he could have an impact, even though the station commander showed no interest in him or the other two chaplains. This optimism even encouraged him to move Jessica and their first daughter, Janet, to be with him. This early hope soon fizzled out, with services poorly attended and his efforts to help the pilots falling on deaf ears.

Marcus began to feel more and more disillusioned with life in the RAF. Perhaps it was because he felt he was being moved from pillar to post, or maybe it was simply the nature of trying to minister to an ever- changing flock. He never felt support from the com- manding officers, and it seemed to him that they weren't even paying lip-service to the religious needs of the men and his position. So, having tried to swim against the tide of apathy for two years, he took the brave step of resigning his commission. It is interesting to note, and backs up his feelings about not being regarded as an integral part of the RAF, that not one of the bases at which he was stationed has any record of his time with them. Most even suggested that they had never before been questioned about the history of the churchmen on their base and had no such records to refer to.

To resign from the forces during wartime was a brave thing to do, and it tells us a lot about Marcus Morris. Many others felt the same but kept their heads down and saw it through, but he didn't believe in that sort of behaviour. He did not take the decision lightly and even tried to get a transfer in the hope of finding a CO with a more inclusive policy. His request was denied. He wanted to help people as best he could, and he decided he was unable to do this in the air force. He left the RAF and Benson in April 1943.

The next stop for the young Morris family was St Andrew's Church in Weeley. Lying ten miles to the east of Colchester, Weeley was, and still is, a small village that you could easily drive through without really noticing it. It is probably best known for the Black Boy pub and its apocryphal place in the history of Dick Turpin. It became a place where Marcus established much of the style of ministry that he would take to his last parish, St James's. It also saw the arrival, in November 1943, of their second child, Kate.

Not for the first time, and certainly not for the last, money was tight for the vicar. It got so tight that he turned the land around the Weeley vicarage into a veritable market garden, growing vegetables, rearing fowl and keeping a goat, a pig and even a cow. Never mind vicar, he was turning himself into Noah. These efforts must have seemed strange to his parishioners, but as there was a war on he was probably not the first to respond to the government's urgings to dig for victory. But still, cash was short and eventually, and quite bizarrely even, he took a job on a production line at a factory in nearby Colchester.

Before long the parish church council realised that having a vicar who was running a farm and working in a factory was not necessarily in the best interests of the churchgoers, and while they pondered how to increase his stipend they made him a gift of a not insubstantial sum, which enabled him to buy a car. At this time he was also teaching, so at the very least the vehicle allowed him to get from one job to the next a little quicker. When he slept is a mystery.

In between all the hard work, Marcus somehow had time to encourage the worst of the village gossips. In any small community there are bound to be petty jealousies and gripes, and not everyone in Weeley was won round to the vicar's ways, which included, among other things, drinking in the Black Boy with his parishioners. As he'd shown in the RAF, he was of the opinion that the followers of Christ were probably already in the church, and to reach folk beyond those he should go to *their* place of worship. It was not for his visits to the pub that Marcus found himself in deep water, though. There were rumours of his getting too close to some of the women in the parish, and word quickly spread. The gossiping got so bad that he even addressed it in a sermon, where

The cover of the first *Eagle* dummy, produced on Frank Hampson's kitchen table in Southport, Lancashire, 1949.

Chaplain Dare. Dan as a vicar in the first dummy.

The recently discovered second dummy, which surfaced in an auction house in Cirencester, Gloucestershire, spring 2008.

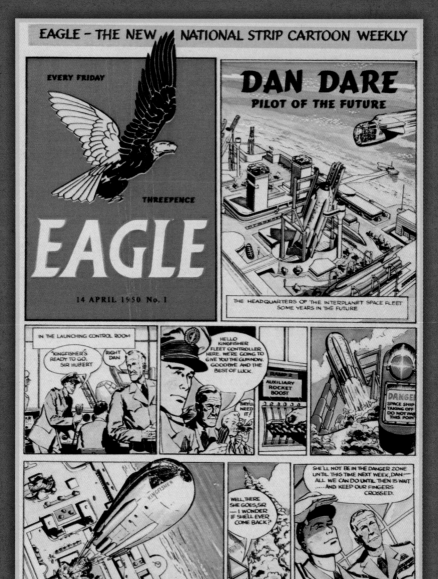

The cover of the first issue of *Eagle*.

'Project Nimbus' begins, and Frank Bellamy, succeeding
Frank Hampson as lead artist, changes everything.

After ten years with Dan Dare as the cover star the 1960s started swinging . . .

. . . and the cover of *Eagle* was rarely the same for long.

More Grand Prix thrills with Lightning Stormm inside

EAGLE

The modern paper for the modern boy

April 26th, 1969. Vol. 20. No. 17
EVERY WEDNESDAY

7d

Australia 10c. New Zealand 1/- (10c). South Africa 10s. Rhodesia 1/-. East Africa 1.00. West Africa 10d.

DAN DARE in THE ROGUE PLANET

THE STORY SO FAR: With 'Mission Cryptos' successfully completed, Dan, Digby, Lex and Flamer—with their pet, Stripey—take off on the fantastically long journey back to Earth. As the Crypt ship commences its amazing flight of five light-years, Dan reveals the grim secret of Lero's scroll.

Continued on Back Page

The *Eagle* comes down to Earth: the final cover.

he attacked the behind-the-back sniping that he felt was working against him.

By early 1945 the whispering campaign had become too much for Jessica, and she left Marcus and the girls to give herself some space and time to get to grips with her life. Not long afterwards Marcus resigned from Weeley and the family, together again, moved back to Southport, the parish of Birkdale to be precise, and what was to be his final church, St James's.

Everywhere that Marcus had worked, he had always encouraged activities beyond the pulpit, and St James's was to be no different. There were obviously the usual money-raising fêtes and the like, but as ever Marcus went further. As his trips to the Black Boy showed, he believed that it was up to him, by any means possible, to bring the message to those beyond the church gates. To this end he founded the St James's Society, which would in time, like an unrestrained ivy, grow beyond all its original boundaries: the film society that it spawned lasted for over thirty years and is still fondly remembered today. The St James's Society was aimed at covering all that a community might be interested in – the arts, politics, dances, there was no real limit – and in this way it flourished and brought many people to the church who had no obvious religious beliefs.

It wasn't long before there was a youth equivalent to the society, with the same aim: of trying to introduce children to a Christian way of life without it being an overt sell. Marcus still remembered the awkwardness he felt at Roby, cycling around the parish like a door-to-door salesman hoping to sell the Bible on the doorstep, and he knew that what he was doing now was a much more successful tactic.

One of the major forms of communication between the local church and its congregation is the parish magazine. In many places this comprised a poorly produced few pages, with content being nothing more than local notices and details of the church's services. In this St James was no different from much of the rest of the country, with its unimaginatively named *Parish Messenger*.

Marcus's first decision was to change the name, and so was born *St James's Magazine*. The editorial in the first renamed issue made it clear to the readers that Marcus wanted to get their involvement in the magazine. While his sermons were his chance to preach to his flock, the magazine should involve a dialogue that went both ways.

As well as encouraging parishioners to participate, Marcus was very successful at getting contributions from well-known and respected luminaries from disparate spheres of the wider world. These included the writer C. S. Lewis, the politician Harold Macmillan and the cricketer Learie Constantine.[*] Not all in the same issue, however.

As the scope and distribution of the magazine grew, so did Marcus's ambitions. In December 1946 he changed the name again, and so appeared for the first time *The Anvil*, with a new design to accompany the new name. The cover was designed by Edward Lancaster and showed a typical Birkdale skyline as viewed through what looks like a church window. Marcus wrote in his opening editorial: 'The new title is not original, but it

---

[*] Learie Constantine helped Marcus out again in the *Eagle* by putting his name and expertise to a series of cricket instructionals, which started in Issue 1.

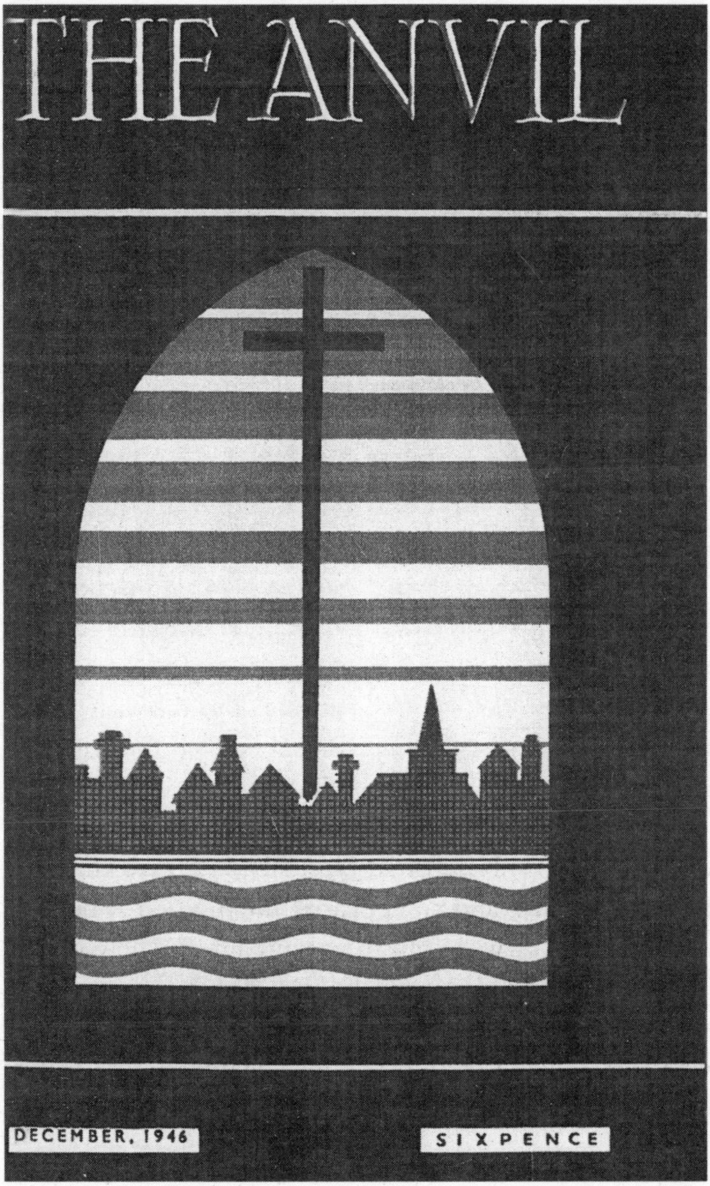
THE ANVIL
DECEMBER, 1946
SIXPENCE

does express better than most names the aims of this magazine. The truth of Christianity has to be hammered out by hard work and thought into a shape which means something in the modern world.' His expressed hope was that 'parishioners adopt it as their magazine through which they can speak'. His ambitions for the publication were way beyond what other vicars would have, but this first issue was a modest affair, with twenty-four pages padded out by generic content shared with other parishes. There was even a letter from a certain Jessica Morris in which she described how northern children were helping to re-educate German youths.

Within the first few weeks Marcus managed to include a discussion on Christianity written by the renowned author Dorothy L. Sayers. The generic content had gone and the pages began to be spruced up with illustrations to break up the text. There were also reports from the church's junior club, details of the Dramatic Society, and film and book reviews. This all-encompassing approach did not receive universal approval, but Marcus was not afraid to confront his critics. There were several letters published complaining about features that seemingly had nothing to do with religion. His defence was that he didn't 'believe there was any subject that is not the concern of religion'. And to prove the point he introduced a short-story competition, a general knowledge quiz and poetry.

While Marcus's aims were laudable, his venture was simply not paying for itself. In spite of several pages given over to adverts and a cover price of sixpence, the books just would not balance. Many people would have blanched at the sight of the blood-red figures in the accounts, but for Marcus it was a case of not turning back on his principles. He was, as we have seen, used to being in debt by now, and so it did not have the restraining effect it may have had on others. He pushed on.

Some money was raised in the usual Church way, with fairs, fêtes and donations, but for Marcus the only way to make the magazine pay was to widen the circulation. This ambition was limited by paper rationing which meant, without special dispensation, that they could only produce 2,500 copies. The rationing of paper had been introduced during the war and lasted till the early 1950s – maybe they needed the paper to print the ration books for all the other items being restricted! It had a major effect on the publishing industry; even national essentials like the *Radio Times* suffered from this. The *Radio Times* got round it largely by using exceptionally thin paper and making use of an extremely small typeface. Publishing businesses had a ration which they could share out among their various publications, so the smaller the business the more problems the rationing created. Marcus lobbied for support to get a bigger licence, but was blocked at every turn. He received backing from many quarters, both within the Church and without, but although no one could give him the extra ration he needed he didn't give in and continued to try and grow the magazine.

By the summer of 1947 the magazine was being read all over the country. The August issue had a letter from one Dora Kinnings from Devon. The month before had seen an article by E. Vallance Cook on one of Marcus's favourite topics entitled 'The Parson in the Pub'. There was also an article on Britishness by the far-right politician A. K. Chesterton. Again, this was not obviously a religious item and drew criticism for its negative portrayal of Jews in Britain. Marcus was not afraid to be controversial in his push for a wider readership.

January 1948 saw another overhaul of the magazine. *Junior Anvil* began, with a serial adventure written by Geoffrey Trease, who is best remembered for writing historical children's novels. Marcus introduced the adventure 'Wild Holiday' thus: 'For some time we have been wanting to have something for our younger readers. We could hardly have made a better start.' This is the first hint at the type of thinking that would eventually lead to Marcus's creation of the *Eagle*. Keeping the adults happy and interested involved the launch of the rather pompously named Anvil Public Opinion Bureau. The aim was to find out the readers' opinions on a topic and publish a discussion about it. The first thorny issue it tackled was gambling, of which 70 per cent of the readers did not disapprove. This was followed by the more controversial subject of divorce and, quite surprisingly, 78 per cent felt it was justified under certain circumstances.

So *The Anvil* had started getting into the nitty-gritty of everyday life, but Marcus was let down by his usual illustrator and so went in search of a replacement.

Frank Hampson was born on 21 December 1918 in Audenshaw, a small town to the east of, and now consumed by, Manchester. Frank's father Robert was a policeman and before Frank was a year old the family had moved to

Southport, where Robert started walking a beat which included St James's Church, Birkdale.

Frank had an older brother, Eric, who was just one year his senior. In 1927, when Frank was ten, his sister Margaret arrived. Margaret is now a sprightly eighty-three-year-old who still lives in the north-west and fondly remembers both her brothers. 'I was very spoilt by them, being the youngest of three. I was very lucky because both my brothers were older so they used to come home and quite often they were home together on leave when Frank was in the army and Eric was in the merchant navy. They used to both take me out, I mean it must have been a trial for them but they did. Frank used to take me to the pictures or whatever or out for a meal.'

Frank first fell in love with drawing and comics thanks to some Canadian relatives who sent over US and Canadian comics. Through these he would later find a connection with Bruce Cornwell, who would join the *Eagle* in the early days. Cornwell is a Canadian raised in California and grew up on the same comics that Frank's relatives were sending him. As a boy Frank spent hours reading these comics, by artists such as Milton Caniff, John Striebel and Hal Foster. Foster is best known for creating 'Prince Valiant', a strip about a heroic Nordic prince set during the reign of King Arthur that is still running today. Striebel's legacy is Dixie Dugan, a Holly-wood showgirl who first appeared in a couple of novels before 'graduating' into comic-strip form. Caniff gave the world 'Terry and the Pirates', but it is of more inter-est here to note that he also created Dickie Dare. This character was created in 1933 and was based on Flash

Gordon-type stories. Dickie Dare was a pre-teen who imagined himself appearing in the fantastic adventures of heroes such as Robin Hood and those from Arthurian legend.

Reading these sorts of comics, it is no surprise that Frank's early efforts were adventure-type drawings. Using the sheets of typing paper that his father brought home from the police station, Frank would spend hours drawing and made sure to avoid the type of subjects he was forced to do at school: 'flowers in a jam jar'.

Frank's first school was Birkdale Primary on Matlock Road, just a mile away from St James's Church on Lulworth Road. The school was built in 1885. It is still open today and retains the Victorian façade that Frank would have seen during his time there. Its website mentions that they have an archive of logbooks and, strange-sounding to modern schoolgoers, punishment books. Sadly there is no record of Frank's time at the school, which ended in the summer of 1929 when he went on to King George V Grammar School.

According to the record cards that are held at what is now King George V College, Frank entered in September 1929 and left in October 1932, just before his fourteenth birthday. That is all the information held at the college. It ceased to be a grammar school in 1979, and since 1982 has only catered for sixth-formers.

Two dead ends. Finding information out about Marcus Morris's schooldays was relatively easy. The comparison with Frank is indicative of the very different types of schooling they received and the background from which they came.

When he was just thirteen, Frank entered a competition in the *Meccano Magazine*. No record exists of whether he won or not, but from March 1933 his work began to appear on the 'Fireside Fun' page, illustrating the jokes that appeared there. The first one, and thus the first drawing Frank ever got paid for, was titled 'Oh Yeah!'. Not only does the joke not endanger any chuckle muscles, it doesn't even seem to make sense, but here it is anyway:

JOHNNY: 'That's Jones minor; he took six wickets for three in the last match.'

HIRAM D. GINK (just over from U.S.A.): 'Yeah! Wall, I guess I kent see the sense in playing a short-sighted guy like that.'

Frank didn't write the jokes, he just illustrated them; and his artwork, even at the tender age of fourteen and a half, was already distinctive. You can see his signature, 'FH 33', just by the right foot of the pointing character. In a 'A (B)rush Job' the signature is by the lamppost.

Frank would continue to contribute to the magazine until June 1937. His final cartoon was prophetically entitled 'Big Changes'.

BIG CHANGES

His signature has changed and his drawing style has developed, but the jokes are still just as bad.

In the four years since he first appeared in print Frank had left school, and in 1935 began working for the General Post Office, initially as a telegraph messenger and shortly afterwards behind the counter selling postal orders. A pencil and paper were therefore always on hand, and it was not long after he started at the post office that Frank was encouraged to produce work for *The Post,* the organ of the Post Office workers' union.

Whereas his work for the *Meccano Magazine* had been individual frames, for *The Post* he graduated to the form for which he would become famous throughout the comic-reading world, the strip. His first strip appeared on 25 July 1935.

Margaret remembers how Frank was always drawing, and she would often help out. 'We had a three-bedroomed house and one of those rooms wasn't used as a bedroom so he used it like a studio type of thing and I used to go and pose for him for hands and arms and things like that.

I can remember posing for him for hours and hours. I just did it for him. It was just one of the things I did. He just wanted to draw and that was it.' Margaret was thus probably the first to endure the rigours of Frank's perfectionism. Drawing wasn't necessarily in the family blood: 'Eric was more interested in the theatre. He worked for a while behind the scenes at the Garrick Theatre in Southport. He was very interested in symphony concerts. He took me to my first symphony concert and he got me interested in that.'

Frank stayed with the GPO and continued contributing to *The Post* until 1938. Robert encouraged Frank to get some real training and collected together some of his drawings and took them to the local art school. The headteacher was sufficiently impressed to offer Frank the chance to attend life classes whenever was convenient in between his shifts at the post office.

It was around this time that art became a real passion for Frank, and he realised that drawing was something he had to work at. The school was the Victoria College of Arts and Science, and on the advice of the head art teacher Frank now enrolled full-time. On the same course was another young artist named Harold Johns, and the two became firm friends.

Having been at the college for a year, and in receipt of his national diploma of design, the course of Frank's life, and that of most of the young men of Europe, took a detour as the Second World War threw its shadow across the continent. Frank was called up into the Royal Army Service Corps as a truck driver. One of his first experiences of war was to be plucked off the beach at Dunkirk.

Frank desperately wanted to join the RAF, and to this end he went through officer training, achieving the rank of lieutenant, but it was to no avail and he was to stay in the army for the whole of the war. He was working the convoys when Antwerp was captured in early September 1944. Nine years later, in his introduction to *Dan Dare's Space Book*, Hampson referred back to his thoughts from Antwerp:

> On the quays of Antwerp you could watch the birth of space travel. You could watch a rocket being fired, wait as it soared invisibly up, tilted and came hurtling down. And then see the flying dusty wreckage of its murderous end.
>
> Space travel was born in those neat cottonwool lines reaching up into the clear blue winter sky. The lines were,

alas, the first realization of the dreams of the scientists and inventors who had been working for years with little two- and three-foot models. Hitler warped their dreams into ends that were foul and repulsive.

But dreamers have a habit of not giving up. And now the world is on the threshold of the greatest step in its history. Very soon man is going to cross space and explore planets around him as Columbus crossed the Atlantic to America – but at the end of the spaceman's voyage will be twenty million Americas.

With hindsight we can see that Hampson got it slightly wrong, but he was still prescient when he wrote this in 1953. It was eight years before Yuri Gagarin became the first man in space, and sixteen before Neil Armstrong's one small step. When the *Eagle* landed in 1969 (that's the landing module for the first successful moon mission, not the comic) and America won the dash for the moon ahead of the Soviet Union, Bob Hope joked that the victory was achieved because 'our Germans were better than theirs'. The rockets that Hampson saw were German rockets, and after the war it was these very same Germans who were cherry-picked by the United States and Russia to give them a running start in the space race. These men were rocket specialists who, had Hitler listened to them, could have helped Germany to win the war. Fortunately Hitler ignored them until it was too late but their expertise gained during the conflict lifted man off this planet. If these men were visionaries, then certainly in his own way so was Hampson, for he was surely not the only artist to see these rocket trails but he was the only one who extrapolated what he saw and went on to create a world, a universe, where space travel was the norm.

It was while he was undergoing his officer training in south Wales, near Cardiff, that Frank met the future Mrs Hampson. Dorothy Jackson was working in a bank in Cardiff. Sadly, their son Peter cannot recall the exact circumstances of their first meeting: 'He was on an officer training course and they met socially at a "do" of some sort and got married.'

When Frank was overseas he would write to Dorothy, and these missives generally included cartoons of the events he had seen and been involved in. Dorothy collected these in an album.

With the war still raging Frank and Dorothy were married on 7 February 1944; and when the war was over and Frank was demobbed, the young couple moved into a council flat on Drewitt Crescent, Southport.

Frank was still in touch with Harold Johns and, eager to give themselves the best chance of finding paid employment in their chosen field, together they signed up at the Southport School of Arts and Crafts on a further extension and training grant. It wasn't long after the course began that Dorothy informed Frank that she was expecting. Suddenly the need for an income overtook Frank's desire to improve his craft, and so he began to seek out freelance work. He quickly began making something of a name for himself. On 29 May 1948 his winning entry into a competition to design a tourist poster for his home town was published in the *Southport Visitor*. But his extracurricular activities inevitably intruded on his

studies, for which he had received a grant, and so before long some of the lecturers were voicing their concerns about how his lack of attendance might affect his ability to get the qualifications he was after.

Unbeknown to them, and Frank, he was just about to have the meeting that would change his life and make qualifications redundant.

According to *Living with Eagles*, the biography written by Marcus's daughters, it was again the *Southport Guardian* journalist Joe Crossley who acted as the matchmaker for Marcus Morris. Having introduced him to his wife less than a decade earlier, it was Crossley's foresight that led Morris to the next most important partnership of his life. Crossley knew that Morris was looking for new artists to liven up his parish magazine, and suggested he pay a visit to the Southport College of Art and seek out a young man by the name of Frank Hampson.

Alastair Crompton, in *The Man Who Drew Tomorrow*, implies that Marcus was asked by the school secretary to wait till the class was finished – quite right too – and that the formal introduction was made by course tutor Raymond Geering. Crompton goes on to quote Morris regarding the meeting: 'When he came out, we were introduced and we talked. I asked if he would like to do some illustrations for my magazine [*The Anvil*], he said he would, and that was how he began to work for me.'

As Aleksandr Orlov might say, 'Simples.' And so from that moment in early 1948 the two men would work together for over ten years and in doing so would create a comic and a hero that would outlast them both.

The work that Marcus wanted Frank to do on *The Anvil* was quite straightforward initially. He had been let down by his illustrator, but had also been looking for someone to bring more life to the publication, to make it a little more modern and forward-looking. While the content was obviously vital for this, it was also clear that an improved design would help carry that content further. Frank produced many drawings to illustrate articles, but it was his redesign of the front cover that probably had the biggest impact. His first innovation was to have a background of a typical Southport street scene, on top of which was placed the table of contents. At the head of the contents was an actual anvil. If you're going to hammer a point home, you may as well hammer it hard. As was his wont, Marcus introduced the new cover and its artist: 'Our new cover has been designed by Frank Hampson, and we hope you will agree that he has done a fine piece of work which illustrates what *The Anvil* stands for.' Well, if *The Anvil* stood for life in an out-of-the-way seaside town with a bobby keeping guard outside the fishmonger's, then indeed it did.

This cover lasted a short time but because it was a typical Southport scene it placed the magazine too firmly in that town, and, as we know, Marcus was aiming beyond that. He wasn't afraid to deal with controversial or global issues. Learie Constantine was interviewed about the colour bar, and stated that it was as evident in the Church as anywhere else. The march of Communism, the Cold War, the atomic bomb, nothing was outside the realms of *The Anvil*. By 1949 the cover had become a blank canvas on which Frank was able to illustrate or highlight that month's main feature with a single cartoon, not dissimilar in style to those from his days at the GPO. The work was on a par with that of some of the best-known political cartoonists working in the national papers.

Due to his efforts to gain the same national platform as those papers, Marcus's name and that of his *Anvil* had become well established in the minds and on the tongues of the laity and Church folk up and down the land. One such was Chad Varah, later founder of the Samaritans, who at the time was the vicar at Holy Trinity in Blackburn. He too was closely involved with his parish magazine and, being so close to Southport, it was almost

THE ANVIL

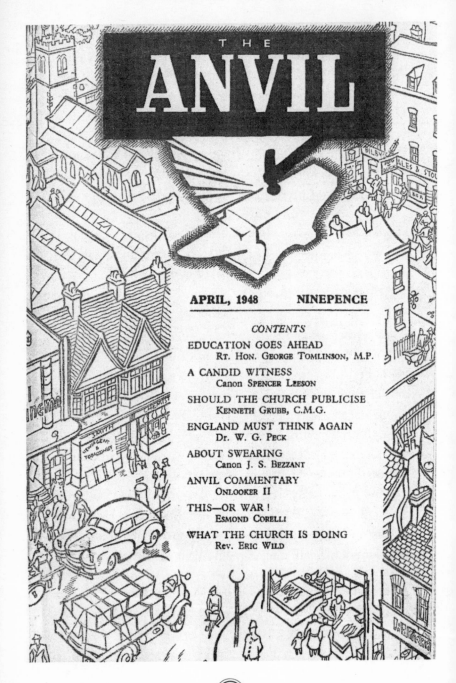

APRIL, 1948   **NINEPENCE**

CONTENTS

inevitable that the two would come into contact. When Varah decided to bring together a group of diocesan editors Marcus was among them. They met in April 1948 to discuss the idea of forming a Society of Christian Publicity (SCP). One of the main aims of the meeting was to help improve all their publications by syndicating between them articles from writers in the public eye whom alone they would be unable to afford. Before the SCP came fully into being they created Interim as a central body for this purpose. In his biography, *Before I Die Again*, Varah recalls that C. S. Lewis was the first writer to be approached. Each editor paid him 7s. 6d. for a piece entitled 'Where the Shoe Pinches'.*

At the first meeting of the society, one of the things Marcus mentioned in his opening speech was other types of periodical that the Church needed. These included a 'strip-cartoon magazine for children'. The SCP took over the publishing of *The Anvil*, as much to help with its debts as anything else. In order to help Marcus keep down costs, Varah began to write for it free of charge, using both his name and various pseudonyms. Under the former he was described as 'Chad Varah, traveller and linguist'.

The day-to-day running of the magazine was not changed by the SCP's involvement, but it did mean that it was no longer under the direct control of St James's. The small parish magazine now hardly had anything

---

* This was a short piece about dealing with your own faults rather than trying to change those in others. Varah got Lewis's permission to rename the piece 'The Trouble with X', and it is under this title that it appears in the collection of Lewis's work *God in the Dock*.

local in it, and its editor was continually thinking about a much larger congregation than that of Birkdale. It was Marcus's constant desire to reach a readership not just beyond his parish but beyond the average churchgoer. On the SCP's takeover, he wrote: 'We hope to see *The Anvil*'s circulation vastly increased so that it becomes the recognised Church magazine for passing on to the outsider.'

A couple of articles in 1949 hint at Marcus's thoughts, or maybe influenced them in the run-up to the creation of the *Eagle*. In May of that year C. O. Rhodes, a regular columnist on anything and everything, wrote, 'The features that bring huge circulations are strip cartoons. These are distinguished neither by wit, humour, plot, characterisation nor aesthetic appeal.' In September R. F. Delderfield wrote an article about the causes of the crime wave among children.

Frank recalled that *The Anvil* was 'running at a great loss' when he joined and that even after he started its fortunes were 'still not very well [and] it became a question of producing something that would make a profit to underpin all the other journals that the society was going to produce'. Marcus and he realised that to do this 'it had to be sold on a national basis. Marcus and I got down to working something out . . .'

'Working something out' makes it sound quite simple, but what this meant was that *The Anvil* was soon to be left behind, and it was not long now until Marcus and Frank went from swimming in the calm coastal waters of Southport to making a splash in the national consciousness.

A couple of examples of Hampson's
line drawings for *The Anvil*

CHAPTER TWO

From *Anvil* to *Eagle*

AT ITS PEAK *The Anvil* had a circulation of 9,000: not bad for a small parish magazine suffering from the restrictions of paper rationing. The first issue of *Eagle* – dated, as fans know by heart, 14 April 1950 – sold all of the 900,000 copies printed.* Not bad for a vicar and a comic-strip novice. They had been working together on *The Anvil* for a couple of years and made a good team, a great team even, but to increase their readership by such a staggering amount beggars belief. How did they manage it? How did they even have the nerve to make the leap from producing a largely text-driven religious-based pamphlet for adults to a cartoon-strip-dominated comic for children? As with most births, it wasn't easy or painless, and it is not 100 per cent certain where conception took place.

Looking for proof in print, it is possible to find various pieces that give clues to the thoughts and plans of Marcus Morris. The first of these can be found in the *Liverpool*

---

* Marcus Morris, *The Best of the Eagle*, Ebury Press, 1977.

Post on 20 December 1948. Under the headline 'Church to Publish Magazines' is an article mainly discussing the formation of the Society for Christian Publicity. This article came nine months after the society formed and is mainly based on quotes from Marcus. It states that the aim of the society is 'to capture the "popular" reading public who seldom see religious periodicals' by appealing to 'all levels of public opinion among non-church-goers'. So far, so Marcus.

This opening gambit is followed by a sentence that is of particular interest to *Eagle* fans. Under a subheading of 'Strip Comics' it states that 'One idea is to attract readers of illustrated weeklies, girls' romances and other cheap fiction. The possibility of running strip cartoons will also be investigated.' This is a clear indication of intent but there is no mention yet of a boys' comic.

Marcus goes on to say, 'Our aim is to produce magazines sufficiently interesting to be bought on their merits, but they will be Christian magazines.' The article confirms that the SCP has taken over *The Anvil* and concludes with Marcus saying of his parish magazine: 'We hope to develop that publication, and as soon as there is a chance we want to produce a news-sheet.'

This article in a major regional paper stirred interest in the nationals, for both the SCP and the publications it may produce. In the *Daily Mirror* of 31 January 1949 one of Marcus's colleagues in the society, the Archbishop of York, Cyril F. Garbett, was quoted appealing for a state campaign to impress on the people the difference between right and wrong. He went on to say that the press, wireless, cinema and posters should be used to 'appeal to all to stamp out petty pilfering and all underhand practices'. What has this got to do with the *Eagle*? The article continues, seemingly on a tangent: 'Strip cartoons featuring people in the Bible will be run in a children's "comic" planned by a group of churchmen and laymen.' The short piece finishes with a quote from Marcus: 'It is time the church was put across in an up-to-date way.'

Less than two weeks later, on 13 February, Marcus penned the article that has gone down in *Eagle* folklore. It was headlined '"Comics" That Take Horror Into the Nursery'. The half-page in the *Sunday Dispatch* became the rallying cry for what was to become the *Eagle*. The article details some examples of the contemporary comics that children were reading without any guidance from their parents. These included stories involving scantily clad female detectives, rape, prostitution, child villains and scenes of graphic murder. The sort of titles he objected to would probably not turn heads today, but you can imagine them giving a vicar in the 1940s a problem. Titles such as the *Phantom Lady* would feature stories such as 'The Soda Mint Killer' or 'The Hooded Horseman'; the first 'graphic novel' was called *It Rhymes with Lust*. As well as these fictional titles there were a lot of true-crime comics. Even those with titles such as *Crime Don't Pay* glamorised violence and the perpetrators of it. The problem with a lot of these American comics is that they were aimed at adults, but because they were comics it was just assumed they were for children. To make his point about the malign influence this sort of content was having on the behaviour of children, Marcus described a case in Canada, which had become known as 'the Comic Book Murder', where two boys aged eleven and thirteen had shot dead a farmer while trying to steal his car. They were avid readers of comics, up to thirty a week, it claimed, and said in their defence that they were copying the behaviour of their favourite character. A Canadian committee on undesirable literature had subsequently discovered that over 20 million 'crime-comics' were printed each month in the USA and Canada.

Going on to discuss his work in the juvenile courts, Marcus quoted two youngsters who had been arrested for a series of burglaries. On hearing one of them tell the other to 'buck up – remember we're tough guys', Marcus had asked them what a tough guy was. The younger of the two, aged eleven, had responded that a tough guy 'has a gun and shoots people and slaps girls in the face' while the older, aged fourteen, said that 'a tough guy knows what he wants, and gets it. And isn't afraid, see – not of cops or anybody.' He sounded more like James Cagney than a child, and this scared Marcus.

In the final section Marcus lays out his distress: 'It sickens and frightens me . . . Children are born hero-worshippers, not born ghouls. They will admire what they are given to admire.' His response can be seen in retrospect as signs of the conception of the *Eagle*: 'I shall not feel I have done my duty as a parson and father . . . until I have seen on the market a genuinely popular "Children's Comic" where adventure is once more the clean and exciting business I remember in my own schooldays.'

As he showed with *The Anvil* in St James's, and in his methods in his previous ministries, Marcus was happy, eager even, to find different ways to spread the word, and in the comic form he was determined to reach the youth of the country. In the *Sunday Dispatch* article he showed how horrified he was by the graphic violence in these mainly US-produced comics being read by the country's youth. One of his main concerns was that parents were not monitoring what their children were reading, and he quoted the latest crime figures to indicate that he believed that the increase in youth crime was a direct result of these influences.

Although it jumps ahead of the story, it is worth looking briefly at what Marcus wrote when *The Anvil* eventually closed in September 1950. He clearly showed his annoyance at his perceived lack of support from the Church: 'The last four years has shown that no magazine of this kind can hope to succeed fully . . . without a much greater measure of support from the clergy and churchpeople generally.' Remember that the following was written when he knew he had a success on his hands, and maybe there was a little gloating when he wrote, 'This decision [to close *The Anvil*] marks the end of an attempt . . . to establish a new kind of popular Christian magazine which would appeal to the man-in-the-street as much as to the man-in-the-pew.' He had now achieved exactly this.

The pieces in the national press stirred up much interest throughout the country, and Marcus received correspondence from concerned parents agreeing with his feelings, and some from even more concerned writers who had continually come up against a brick wall when trying to publish something more in line with what Marcus prescribed.

In spite of the attention his articles aroused, the subsequent clamour for a magazine, and his own stated intentions, Marcus felt that he and Frank would not be able to produce a whole comic; but he did have an idea for a strip cartoon that he hoped to sell to a Sunday newspaper. That idea went by the name of 'Lex Christian', who was to be a vicar working with children in the slums of the East End of London.

They had strong interest in this idea from Terence Horsley, the editor of the *Sunday Empire News*, which at one point in its life had been owned by Edward Hulton Sr, Marcus's contemporary at Brasenose. Life is full of coincidences, avoidable tragedies and unforeseeable consequences, so please excuse what appears to be a tangent.

Terence Horsley fell in love with gliding in the mid-1930s and mixed this passion with fishing. He distributed his time between them, depending on the weather conditions, and even wrote a book on his two favourite pastimes entitled – what else? – *Fishing and Flying*, which was published in 1947. If the riverbanks had been his only sport the history of the *Eagle* could well have been very different or even non-existent.

On 24 April 1949 Horsley died when his glider, an Olympia he had named *The Log of the Wild Goose*, went into a dive caused by damage to the tailplane, which had happened during the launch but gone unnoticed by both Horsley and the ground crew.*

With the champion for the 'Lex Christian' comic strip gone, it could well have been the end of Marcus's

---

* Obituary of Terence Horsley from *The Aeroplane*, 13 May 1949

ambitions. But as we have already seen he was not one to let problems block his path. As always he did not see it as a time for a step back but as a sign that he should aim higher. In his foreword to *The Best of Eagle* he remembers the time immediately after Horsley's death: 'This proved to be a turning point. I still recall a late-night visit to Hampson's house when I told him that we should pack up the idea of doing a single strip for any paper, and that we should be bold and resolute and concentrate our energies on producing an entirely new, original children's paper of our own. He agreed immediately.'*

It seems slightly strange that Marcus should go from thinking they were only capable of producing a strip to having such a firm belief that they could make a whole comic, especially at a time when the person who had shown the most interest in that single strip had gone from the scene. Maybe it was desperation, or maybe, and perhaps more likely, Frank had a strong hand in pushing for something more ambitious.

From his foreword to *The Best of Eagle* it seems that the impetus for a full comic clearly came from Marcus. But from his discussions with Alastair Crompton, reported in *The Man Who Drew Tomorrow*, Frank stakes his claim as the main driving force. He is reported as saying that Marcus, an unnamed journalist and he had a meeting shortly after Horsley's death and agreed that the best way to make money was through a boys' magazine. Marcus, he goes on, tried unsuccessfully to get some financial support for the idea while he, Frank, was

---

* Marcus Morris, *The Best of the Eagle*.

convinced that they needed some dummy copies to gain real backing. Frank says that he called Marcus to say so, and received the response to go ahead if he thought it was the right thing to do. It is here that, in Frank's memory, the *Eagle* is born.

Seeking inspiration for the type of comic he wanted to produce, he thought back to his pre-war reading:

> In particular Milton Caniff's [work] was so accurate in its detailing of aircraft and of ships of every kind of furniture. Everything that was in the thing was fully detailed. And this appealed to me very much. When we had the problem of producing a boys paper that appealed to boys aged 12–14 this was the kind of work that came to mind. [In US Comics] English people found the characters were grotesque, and the speed of the strips and the inferences in them were much too sophisticated for an English audience. I had to slow the speed down and at the same time make it very English.
>
> The *Eagle* developed out of the dummy I produced, virtually single-handed, on my own dining-room table. In fact I produced dummies of the first three issues of the *Eagle*. I still had ambitions to work as a freelance illustrator but Marcus made it clear he needed me . . . so I threw in my lot, as it were, with the Society [for Christian Publicity], Marcus and the *Eagle*.

While this difference of opinion – or maybe it is just a difference of memory – will never satisfactorily be settled, there is one thing that no one seems to dispute. It was Dorothy, Frank's wife, who came up with the name of the comic. Chad Varah remembers that an early idea for the comic's name was *Junior Post*. Bearing in mind that *Eagle* was eventually published by Hulton Press, this name must have been picked to forge a link with another Hulton publication, the *Picture Post*. Fortunately Dorothy stood up and was counted when required. She was in the background during the Alan Vince interview with Frank and interjected every now and then: 'I began to toy with some names. I thought about the Reverend Marcus Morris, the church, the Bible, then it came to me. You know the lecterns they have in churches? Those large impressive eagles, well, there it was *EAGLE*! It seemed an ideal name.'

As for Dan Dare himself, there would seem to be some dispute about who had this idea too. Some early comic-book encyclopedias even failed to credit Frank Hampson at all, not that they credited Marcus either. *Living with Eagles* gives the impression that Marcus at one point claimed to have come up with the idea of Lex Christian the East End vicar alone, and this is backed up in *The Best of Eagle*, where Marcus states that 'Before starting on the *Eagle* I had the idea of an exemplary character, Lex Christian.' In *Living with Eagles* his daughters state that he wrote in 1958 that he came up with the idea of Dan leaving the streets of London to patrol the airways, inspired, they suggest, by reading C. S. Lewis's *Perelandra*. This was the second book in C S. Lewis's cosmic trilogy and was published in 1943. Interestingly *Perelandra* was republished in 1953 under the title 'Voyage to Venus'. *Living with Eagles* gives no indication as to where Morris made this claim, and it seems to be a piece of post-rationalisation.

Surely Dan Dare is a heady mix of those characters that Frank read in his youth, starting with Striebel's Dixie Duggan. Frank had had an idea for a female detective, Dorothy Dare, stewing for a while. While Dixie was a showgirl, she was a strong female character and could well have been the influence for Dorothy. Hal Foster's heroic Prince Valiant gets added into the mix, with a pinch of the Flash Gordon derring-do of Dickie Dare. If CSI took on the case, there would be more than enough evidence to show Frank's fingerprints all over the place. He does admit that Lex Christian was something he worked on *with* Marcus, and so it seems clear that the vicar was the final piece of the jigsaw that Hampson put together to create the Pilot of the Future. To quote from Chad Varah's autobiography: 'Christian heroes were transferred to the back page of the magazine and Hampson came up with Dan Dare.'

So it is not in doubt that Frank created Dan, but it is probably equally true that if Morris and Hampson had not met and worked together, the *Eagle* would not have been created and Dan Dare would have had nowhere to exist, or certainly not in the form we know him. As Frank himself admitted, it was Marcus's need for him that kept him tied in to the whole project in spite of his desire to work as a freelance, so they both deserve the plaudits; one for being the creator and the other for enabling the circumstances for that creation to flourish. Varah again: 'None of his [Marcus's] dreams would have been possible but for his discovery of a brilliant artist in the same town . . . namely Frank Hampson. Frank was not only the most talented artist

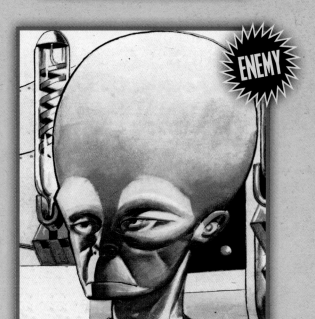

Dan's greatest enemy, The Mekon, and two of his most enduring allies, one from either end of the universe's social scale: Groupie and President Kalon.

Some allies started as enemies, some as strangers and some were simply family. Clockwise from top left: Sondar, Prof. Ivor Dare and The Dapon.

ENEMY

Dan was never afraid to move up a weight
division, or ten, here seen battling Gogol.

They came from near and far. Clockwise from top left: Laslo Romanov, UN Prime Minister, Tharl and Volstar.

ENEMY

ALLY

ALLY

Sometimes it was easier than others to work out who was on your side: the Selektrobots, Cosmobe and, bottom right, Lero, the Man from Nowhere.

A rogue's gallery of Dan's nightmares. Clockwise from top left: Blasco, the Rootha, Vora and Zel.

Frank Hampson's favourite baddies.

Ally, enemy or both? Galileo McHoo forced
Dan to go in search of his past.

but also one who could tell a story compellingly in a series of pictures, and for a story about the future could devise spaceships and other equipment which had not been invented.'

Mainly on his own, but with some help from Harold Johns, Frank put the dummies together. The amazing thing is that they are not that different from what would eventually be featured in the first issue. The quality of the drawing was all there; maybe some of the strips did not quite match up to 'Dare', but for what was in effect a one-man production the dummy was a high-class product. As can be seen from its cover, it had much of what would appear in the very first issue. Dan Dare, of course, was there, as was Frank's tale of St Paul, 'The Great Adventurer'. 'Secret City' did make it through but was renamed after its hero, Rob Conway.

The front page acted as an advert for the whole comic; it had not yet been decided that the 'Dan Dare' strip would be on the cover and page 2. Neither Joe nor Ernie made it all the way through to 14 April 1950, and while Rob Conway was there Frank hastily handed him over to Greta Tomlinson and Harold Johns, who took him up a cul-de-sac with a trip to Tibet. They quickly realised that they couldn't develop him and he was dropped after fifteen weeks. It shows how bad 'Rob Conway' was that it didn't even outlast the reviled 'Seth and Shorty'.

So finally they had a product with a totemic strip to the fore and much more inside. It was time to find a publisher. As has been said elsewhere, it is easy to build the best mousetrap in the world, it is a whole other matter to make people buy it. It was Marcus who had the onerous task of hawking the sample copies around the publishing houses of London.

Marcus's trips up, down and around Fleet Street and the tiring train journey back up north have gone down in *Eagle* folklore and many aficionados can recite by heart each person or company who had the chance to say yes but chose to say no. Before we relive that journey, it is also worth noting that at around this time Chad Varah had been transferred down to London, to St Paul's Church. Not the cathedral; he was based in Clapham, south London. He acted for a time as Marcus's representative down south; and at some point during the trials and tribulations described below Marcus got so desperate that he asked Varah to see if the *Church Times* was interested in taking it on. Sadly, or maybe not so, they weren't interested, but they did like *The Anvil* and bought the rights to it. This injection of cash helped keep Marcus afloat and thus saved the *Eagle* at a critical moment.

It reads like one of Dan Dare's adventures as our hero journeys alone through the mean and unforgiving universe of Fleet Street's publishing houses. Along the way he meets allies: it was Hulton Press that he approached first and which, without saying yes or no itself, sent him on his first mission to see John Myers at J. Arthur Rank. He comes into dead ends: Myers passed him on to Montague Haydon at Amalgamated Press, who said no thanks. There are red herrings: Mike Wardell at the *Sporting Record* seemed interested but unsurprisingly couldn't help. He travels from place to place, always hearing the same thing. Sir Neville Pearson of Newnes, the US publisher Boardman's, John Walter of *The Times*, the *Daily*

Telegraph's proprietor Lord Camrose, all said the same thing: 'No thanks.'

It seemed that as one door slammed in his face, another was closing on his back. The journeys back to Southport were times when Marcus could think. He had sermons to write, debts to pay, other leads to consider, but he was beginning to paint himself into a corner. As long as he kept trying to sell the *Eagle* he was getting further and further into debt, and it got to the point when if he hadn't found a buyer he could well have faced the embarrassment of going bankrupt and dragging the church down with him. Not the Church: the debts were big, but not that big.

Like a mountaineer trapped on the end of a rope down a pothole, he had to keep on travelling down in the hope that his feet would touch solid ground before the rope ran out. He was a man on a mission, but it was a mission that could well have been his last.

Lutterworth Press, who fifty years later would publish Marcus's biography by two of his daughters, was very interested but could not see how it could overcome the problem with paper rationing. To make it work they needed to print a lot, but they had used up their allowance on other publications. The darkest hour is just before the dawn, a cliché but true. As the end of the rope approached, with no ground in sight, Marcus went back to where he had started: Hulton Press. While they had passed him on to another publisher they had never actually said the fatal word: 'No.'

He managed to secure a meeting with Ronnie Dickenson, an assistant general manager at Hulton. Dickenson flicked through the dummy and asked Marcus to wait while he showed it to his bosses, John Pearce and Maxwell Raison. Marcus was called in to meet the general managers, who requested that they be allowed to keep hold of the dummy for a few days.

Marcus left the office and headed back to Birkdale. It must have been a long and dark journey, for he had now exhausted every possibility. A few days passed and then like manna from heaven a telegram arrived at the vicarage. It was from John Pearce, and it was short and to the point: 'Definitely interested. Do not approach any other publisher.' Since he'd already approached them all, this was hardly a problem.

And so it was that after so many rejections there was finally a yes, and Hulton Press became the publisher of *Eagle*. The owner at this time was Edward Hulton, the son of the Edward Hulton who had once owned the *Sunday Empire News*, the first publication to have shown an interest in the Lex Christian strip. Like a moon orbiting a planet, what goes around eventually comes back around. This is also the same Edward Hulton who went to Brasenose College, Oxford, where Marcus was also a student.

CHAPTER THREE

A Star is Born: Dan dares to be the best in the business

AT WRITING SCHOOL, one of the first things they tell you is to write about what you know. By the time Marcus Morris began his move from vicar to publisher he had been a man of the cloth for almost ten years. His father and his father's father had both been in the Church and so it was natural that the first character he created was a vicar. For the strips they showed to Terence Horsley, Marcus wrote the stories and Frank drew them.

Lex Christian was a parson working out of a church in the East End of London. Although Marcus had been a vicar for some time he really didn't have that much experience in a big city, let alone the tough streets of the capital. Maybe this was why the 'Lex Christian' strip had not quite rung true for Horsley. While he had shown much interest in the idea of the strip, he had not given it the green light. Marcus and Frank were still working on changes when Horsley took his fatal flight.

There is no suggestion of a link between Horsley's love of flying and Lex's metamorphosis into a flying padre, but it is surely more than just coincidence. The first step along the way to change must have been Horsley's insistence that the character was not quite working. After much thought he moved from the East End into the fighting services. He kept his dog collar but lost his slightly too obvious name.

Frank described the process of change:

> At first it seemed natural to have a chaplain as a hero. This stemmed from the fact that we were working for a Christian publicity society. Apart from Dorothy Dare I had, with Marcus, worked on an idea aimed at the newspaper market, called Lex Christian. This was not a science-fiction hero; he was very down-to-earth, dealing with the problems of the present. But we soon realised that this would be too limiting for a national paper, so when Dan was finalised it was a *pilot* of the future, which had an apt double meaning.

As an interesting aside, Frank also said to Vince:

> When we got around to planning *Eagle* we were faced with two choices for the front-page feature: one, a western, and two, a science-fiction strip . . . The western was always a big favourite with young and old alike. I felt it was a little limited, for a front page, so I decided on the science-fiction strip. If you wanted to create a completely new set of conditions and 'types' you just go to a different planet. The scope was so wide. Then again in 1950 I was sure that before long space travel would be a reality, and kids deserved a much more optimistic view of rockets and science.

A strong argument for sci-fi as a front-pager, but after a short pause Frank continued, laughing: 'Apart from that I just didn't want to draw all those horses!'

The western of course was fitted in to the *Eagle*, initially in the shape of 'Seth and Shorty'. This was not signed by writer or artist and was never well liked but lasted sixteen weeks. Frank's assertion that westerns were always popular proved to be true when Charles Chilton's 'Jeff Arnold and Riders of the Range' was plucked from the radio and developed into a strip. It proved more successful than its predecessor and ran until the early 1960s. As for Frank not wanting to draw all those horses? Anyone with a passing knowledge of the 'Venus' story will remember that he ended up doing just that for the finale.

So Dorothy Dare was going to be a detective, and this idea was on the back burner in the Hampson kitchen (Frank did most of his work on the kitchen table), while Lex Christian was preaching in the streets of London. The first thing to go was the name, but he was still a parson, as can be seen in the first dummy. The new name came partly from Dorothy Dare and it has been suggested by Peter Hampson that one of the factors in favour of Dan Dare was Dorothy Hampson's admiration for the hymn 'Dare to be a Daniel'. You can take the parson out of the church, but you can't take the church out of the parson, even when he eventually loses his vicar's garb.

Looking at the lyrics to the hymn, you can almost see them as a blueprint for Dan Dare's character and the adventures on which he embarked:

Standing by a purpose true,
Heeding God's command,
Honor them, the faithful few!
All hail to Daniel's band!

Dare to be a Daniel,
Dare to stand alone!
Dare to have a purpose firm!
Dare to make it known.

Many mighty men are lost,
Daring not to stand,
Who for God had been a host
By joining Daniel's band.

Many giants, great and tall,
Stalking through the land,
Headlong to the earth would fall,
If met by Daniel's band.

Hold the Gospel banner high!
On to vict'ry grand!
Satan and his hosts defy,
And shout for Daniel's band.

Philip B. Bliss, 1873

Marcus was, of course, a religious man; Frank by his own admission was not, but he had still been involved in Church activities for a while now due to his work on *The Anvil* and 'I admired him [Marcus] and was infected by his desire to . . . publish morality.' And so, one way or another, the church wine found its way into Dan Dare's blood.

The first dummy copy of the *Eagle* that Marcus took down to London had, as we saw in Chapter 2, 'Dan Dare of the Interplanet Patrol'. He wore what could be described as RAF colours but still quite clearly has his black shirt and dog collar. It is no real surprise that at this stage he looks more like the Revd Marcus Morris, thinner than the Dan Dare we now know, and not yet with his trademark eyebrows. The story, on pages 2 and 3, is titled 'Chaplain Dan Dare', and the plot is pretty much that which would eventually find its way into the first comic, just under a year later. The only difference is that Dan is not a pilot, but is called to an emergency meeting with the Interplanet Patrol's controller, Sir Hubert (Dan's eventual commander-in-chief) in all but name. At the meeting are the four best pilots in the world.

Every now and then, like the Piltdown Man, a discovery is made that turns the world on its head. In 2008 Dominic Winter Book Auctions put up for sale a decade's worth of volumes of *Eagle* and *Girl*. The Cartoon Museum in London won the bidding, and their joy was doubled when they found among the lot a previously unseen dummy. This was much more similar in style to what would be the eventual first issue. This dummy is for a second issue and speculation has it that it was produced to convince the Hulton bosses that the team could produce quality week in week out. Therefore it may have been created after Hulton's initial interest but before they signed on the dotted line – although Frank claimed to have produced three dummies before Marcus even went down to London. Either way, the changes are interesting in highlighting the development of the magazine in general, but they actually show a greater amount of change in Dan Dare.

As this is the second episode, the 'Dan Dare' pages are an early version of what would appear on 21 April 1950. The intriguing thought is that if the team had been asked to show they could produce work on a regular basis and Frank said he made three dummies, surely there must be a dummy of issue three lurking out there somewhere.

Looking more closely at this second dummy we find that Dan has obviously swapped his vicar's collar for flying gear and overtaken those other four flyers to become the star of Space Fleet, but he has changed physically as well. He has filled out a little; his face is more masculine – his jaw even looks stronger – and his eyebrows have got much closer to acquiring their signature flourish. Oh, and, very importantly, Digby was at his side. Yes, he had definitely become Dan Dare – Pilot of the Future.

Before moving on to see who else would accompany Dan into the future it is important to take a moment to look at the other iconic image that would feature on the front cover, the masthead. In this second dummy the front cover was now almost what would become the standard for the first ten years of the comic, with the larger first frame of the story at the top right and for the first time the single red panel at the top left, although this was still not the final version. At this point it is called *The Eagle*, rather than *Eagle*, and the typeface is not what readers would see on the real first issue. For that Marcus Morris turned to the typographic designer Ruari McLean.

In his autobiography, *True to Type*, McLean explains that Morris had initially been in contact with him to produce personal stationery. McLean had obliged and the two men had stayed in touch. On one of his trips down to London with the first *Eagle* dummy, Marcus had shown it to McLean and indicated that he would like to try and publish it himself. McLean did not encourage this idea. When, a few months later, Morris informed him that Hulton had taken on the magazine, McLean felt that his involvement had ended as they had their own people, at Curwen Press, to do the type design.

He goes on to explain that for some reason the job was not done by Curwen's top man, Oliver Simon, but by an underling who was no more than competent. Marcus showed what they had produced to McLean. They both agreed that it lacked inspiration and Morris asked McLean if he could do better. The eagle that would fly across the masthead had been drawn by this time, by Hampson: 'The big black and yellow one? Yes, I did that. Put on the red background it was easily recognisable to the readers,' but it was McLean who would suggest the typeface called Tempest. This font had been designed by Berthold Wolpe in 1936 when he was still working in Germany. By the late 1940s he was in London and was asked by McLean to draw the word 'EAGLE' in his font. Hulton liked it, agreed to use it, and McLean was taken on as typographic designer to the comic. Frank Hampson's eagle and Berthold Wolpe's EAGLE were thus united and would sit alongside Dan Dare on the cover.

Having created the central character, it was equally important to make sure that those gathered around him formed a strong team, 'Daniel's band' as the hymn refers to them. As we have seen with Hampson and Morris, two heads are better than one, and no superhero is complete without his sidekick. In the first frame of the second dummy we are introduced to Albert Fitzwilliam Digby, referred to as Dan's batman. The Batman, the DC Comics character, had already surfaced by this time, but a batman was the personal servant that officers in the services had. It would be nice to think that in calling Dan's partner his 'batman' there was a subtle suggestion that Dan reigned above the Caped Crusader.

Digby was not really a batman in the old sense, even though in the first episode of the actual comic, and in later ones too, he is seen acting as a servant to Dan, in this case bringing him his hearty breakfast of vitamin blocks. If that had been his true and only role he would have ended up being the equivalent of Alfred Pennyworth and not journeyed with Dan on his travels. He actually ended up becoming a bit of a cross between Alfred and Robin. Physically he is the opposite of Dan. Almost a foot shorter, with white hair and a round, friendly, almost comical face, he comes across as a friendly uncle type. This is further emphasised by him being around ten years older than Dare. He is, of course, loyal and has a strange bravery which comes through in spite of himself. He would do anything for Dan and often puts his life on the line.

As well as being Dan's constant companion, Digby played an important role for the reader. Although he was actually rather intelligent (how else could he have been a space pilot?) he could always be relied upon to ask the stupid question. The strip, in line with Marcus's early aims, was not just pure entertainment; it had to be educational too. The important thing was that this element, like the religious one, had to be subtle. What better way to put information over than to get one of the characters to ask about it? Digby also offered light relief even in times of the greatest stress, and could always be relied upon to bring a smile to those around him.

Sir Hubert Guest, Dan's commander-in-chief, also appeared in the first dummy, and the first comic. At that early stage it was not obvious that he would be so much a part of the team. While Dan is the chief pilot there is never any doubt that Guest is the boss. Dan may not always agree with the old feller, but he would never show a lack of respect. Guest has had a lifetime in Space Fleet and flew missions with Dan's father. He is tall and distinguished, with a ramrod-straight back and a will of iron.

It wasn't until *Eagle* no. 5 that members four, five and six appeared. The first of these were Hank Hogan and Pierre Lafayette. The inclusion of these two foreigners was an important part of the dynamic and also reflected Frank's views on the world, the United Nations and multiculturalism. '[That was] something I was very keen on, you'll recall the commander of the UN force that landed on Venus was a negro . . .' Frank was always a supporter of the UN: 'Trouble is it doesn't seem to work . . . it did in Dare. It's like the Americans, I get on with those I've met . . . it's their government that worries me.' It is worth remembering that these comments are from an interview in early 1974, just six months or so before President Nixon was forced to resign due to the Watergate scandal. It seems that once again Frank was ahead of the times.

Hank and Pierre generally come as a pair and offer similar contrasts to Dan and Digby. Hank is the blond, tall, all-American, gung-ho guy from Texas, although we know he is not just a jock and has smarts too because he wears glasses. Pierre is the sophisticated Frenchman but, having a similar frame to Digby, can also be quite funny. While these two seemed to complete the band of merry men, there was one final member of this initial team, who turned up last and who really got the pulse racing.

To quote from the other characters upon the appearance of Professor Peabody: 'Gosh, Jumpin' Jets, Sufferin' Cats, A WOMAN!' When the group of five old comrades sat around discussing the boffin who had been foisted upon them by the world government for the trip to Venus, none of them had expected the professor to be a female and it probably wasn't only Sir Hubert who was shocked by and opposed to her inclusion. Like his, though, all objections were crushed.

It was only a comic strip, but this really was a big boost for women's liberation. Even though women had played a vital role in the Allied victory, they were never directly involved in the fighting and certainly not on the front line, but here was a leading female character in the biggest comic of the day taking her place among the boys.

It was a bold and innovative move and maybe harked back to Frank's idea of Dorothy Dare. He wasn't able to have a woman as the main character but in Jocelyn Mabel Peabody he created a strong and important individual who used her brains to help out the team on many occasions and was also incredibly brave.

This stab at equality was not limited to the characters

in the strip. The team producing Dan Dare had three women – Joan Porter, Greta Tomlinson and Jo Thomas – who were as important as the men and shared their duties on an equitable basis. While the war had seen many women take on traditional male jobs to cover the loss of workforce caused by the call-up, this trend had not continued after the war. Returning soldiers needed employment and many women who had been fully employed during the hostilities returned to their homes. Thus it was against the trend that the studio was split almost 50:50 between the sexes.

It may not all have been about equality though. Frank once said of Peabody: 'She was there to be rescued.' Hmm. But he went on: 'I didn't want to produce a strip without a female. I struck a blow for Women's Lib. She was shown as a very clever, attractive young lady. It [Peabody's inclusion] also paved the way for a few arguments between her and Sir Hubert – a nice human touch.' A further thing to consider is that Peabody, based on Greta Tomlinson, was about the same age as Frank's sister Margaret and Sir Hubert was based on his father Robert. The special relationship between the Prof and Guest must therefore, for Frank, have had elements of what he saw between his father and sister. The friendly sniping between the two never got nasty and covered up Sir Hubert's deep sense of caring for Peabody's welfare, and from her side a strong respect for the older man mixed with a need to rebel. Frank often said that he wanted his characters to look as if they had 'a history, families back home', and surely here is a prime example of how he used his own history and family to imbue that degree of truth in how he drew them, how they behaved to each and to the world around them. It is interesting to see how often they not only end up together, as in the third rocket in the first story, but how often when there are other people in a scene they are put in a frame together, always backing each other up.

If one looks at successful television series now, it is clear how this model of six or seven contrasting but complimentary characters is used to make up the core group, from the obvious example of *Star Trek* all the way through to shows like *Friends* or *Blake's Seven* and *Cold Feet*. It is enough for there to be conflict and drama, but not so many characters that you lose track of who's who, where they are and what they're up to.

Over the years others were added to the Dan Dare team, and some of the original six took time on the sidelines, but for most *Eagle* fans it is this group that epitomises all that was great about the stories. The beauty of this bunch is that even though they were all adults, there was someone for every young reader to associate themselves with. Frank felt the truth of the characters was important: 'I was determined to produce a real character and a consistent character, for the front page. Someone people would notice.'

A lot of families lost a father, or a son, an uncle or a brother during the war, in many cases the main man of the house, and even though Dan Dare appeared five years after the end of the conflict, there were a lot of kids in search of that vital missing role model. Dan Dare filled that hole. He was strong, brave and honest. Who wouldn't have wanted him to be their dad?

Having a strong core of characters is, of course, important, but equally so are the adventures on which they are sent, and for a new comic it was absolutely vital that the readers were hooked in week one so that they had to come back for more. That first week saw the very future of the planet in jeopardy. One of the clever things that was done was to put the reader in the same situation as the protagonists. When the *Kingfisher* launches and heads for Venus on the same mission as two previous failed attempts, Sir Hubert points out that 'She'll not be in the Danger Zone until this time next week.' And you, dear reader, will have to wait a week as well. Will you be able to bear it?

Reading that now in a world where we can have anything, everything we want instantly, it is easy to miss the significance of that teasing statement. When we read old copies of the comic now we can devour the whole story of 'The Voyage to Venus' in one sitting. We don't have to wait a week to find out the fate of *Kingfisher*, but on 14 April 1950 the reader would have just those two pages. Unlike the overstimulated, short-attention-span children of today, a schoolboy (or girl) would enjoy poring over the two pages for hours and hours. So for that young reader to feel that they were playing the same waiting game as Sir Hubert, Dan and Digby must have been thrilling. And we haven't even thought about the creation of a world where it is commonplace to fly to Mars.

The first frame of the first comic is in itself a big hook. Flying in at speed from the right of the frame is what looks like a small spaceship; on the launchpad is an impressive rocket, with another ready to launch in the background and a third in dock to the fore. The space station looks clean and ultra-modern and is right by a beach being lapped by an inviting green-blue ocean. We know now that this is Southport beach, so the ocean is in fact the very cold Irish Sea, but let's not allow that to spoil the view.

The Headquarters of the Interplanet Space Fleet some years in the future, the caption announces. We don't know it yet but this story is set some forty-five years into the future, but here is a world where space travel is the norm and the buildings positively shine in the late-evening sun. In 1950s Britain many of the country's major cities were still scarred by the bombing raids of the recent war and in spite of the fact that we had been on the winning side life was no picnic. Escapism in pure and simple form was offered by 'Dan Dare' in that very first frame, but the clever element of the first story, which was only called 'Voyage to Venus' after the event, was that it was to do with food shortages. The aim of the voyage to Venus was to find another planet capable of producing enough food to feed the growing population of Earth. Resources here were insufficient and the planet and its population were in jeopardy. Everyone's daily diet was supplemented by the same 'Vitamineats' Digby delivers to Dan in episode one.

In the real world, rationing was not only still in place after the war, it was in some cases even harsher than during hostilities. For instance bread, normally available during the war, was rationed from 1946 to 1948. Confectionery rationing was not to end until February 1953, and sugar was limited until September the same year. Rationing did not end completely until 1954. Our hero makes light of the problems with some typical British gallows humour. For readers still suffering from rationing it must have been fascinating to see how the very same problems of food shortages might be solved in the future. Frank again: 'I . . . felt that young people were getting a rough deal in those years so soon after the end of the war. Everything was so pessimistic, what with the bomb and all . . . I wanted to give them something that made the future more helpful, in human terms.'

Terry Jones, most famous as one of the Monty Python team but also a massive Dan Dare fan, remembers life just after the war:

> I can remember also it was very difficult to heat the house. I remember waking up in the winter – there was no central heating, of course, there were no cavity walls – and I remember not [just] having ice on the inside of the window, but ice on the walls.
>
> I can remember rationing, but that's just what you did. It was odd for our parents. I remember when they stopped the national loaf: instead of having white you had this loaf that had a grain in it, but it was better for you. But I remember the moment when my mum said we could get real white bread again. Which has got everything milled out of it!

As the first week's instalment ends Dan receives a call to come to HQ on his 'personal radio', to all intents and purposes a bluetooth phone. And so Dan and Digby hurtle to HQ in their 'jepeet' (bluetooth was invented in the 1990s but we still await the invention of this particular vehicle, which Hampson admitted was a rip-off of the Chrysler Airflow) to discover the fate of *Kingfisher*.

Terry Jones remembers the impact of discovering *Kingfisher*'s fate:

> What I really remember is the horror of the second or third week, when you'd seen all the introductory stuff of Hubert Guest and the World Government and rockets taking off, and it was so cinematic. He was using cinema in his head in the way he did close-ups and long shots. He could have directed film like anything, and I think that gave me the feeling for film in a way. But it was the horror of the blown-up *Kingfisher*, there was that moment of 'Oh God, what's happened to them?' And it felt very daring to have that in a comic.

We've seen technology beyond our imagination, and beyond the limits of 1950s inventors; we've met our hero and his sidekick; but they seem just like normal blokes. They could be our dad or uncle, and they have the same problems as us: not enough food. In just two pages of stunning colour we are hooked. Ah yes, that's the final trick to grab our attention. The colour, the beautiful colour. Although the printing process was not quite up to speed in capturing Hampson's creation, it was still enough to knock spots off the competition. It was the colour and the detail that did it. Just look again at the very first frame; there really is so much in it that every time you go back to it you find something new. It is no coincidence or surprise that Frank insisted on that frame being so large and spent so much time producing it.

You can see how it would have been possible, easier even, to do it less well and still have the flavour of the story. But without the four rockets, the spaceship, the hovercraft on the quay, the waves, the totally realised buildings, the car park, even the shrubbery, we would have a commonplace strip. The greatest filmmakers through the years have attempted to make each frame a masterpiece of composition so that it could stand alone as a single image, and this is what Hampson does. He doesn't just want us to read the strip, follow the stories and fall in love with the characters. He has higher ambitions. He wants us to, and makes us, go back time and time again to each frame and marvel at what he has created.

When he created a rocket or a piece of technology, he would not be content just to draw the outer shell. For it all to work he had to know the details of what went beneath the skin, even though the reader might never see it. He has stated that he wanted his 'characters to look as if they had a history, families back home, blood pressures', and the same was true of the technology. He would spend hours drawing these inner workings; they might be used at a later date, they might not, but it was this attention to the little things that made what we did see so amazing and why it has survived through the years. It is this longevity for which he strived. All this attention to the detail of each frame may lead one to think that all Hampson cared about was the art, but in fact the opposite was true. 'My big ambition was never so much to draw a good picture but more to produce a good story. The kind of story a boy would read once, twice, three times – and still get something out of it.'

The final element in the first adventure, and those that followed, was, of course, the enemy. Drama is created by tension, and so, as strong as you want to make your hero, you have to have an enemy for him that is of equal or even of seemingly slightly greater strength. In this the first tale it is Dan's never-to-be-fully-defeated nemesis, the Mekon. The name, according to Frank, derives from machinery and this is why the Mekon is driven purely by logic as a machine would be. 'This was arrived at by thinking about something mechanical . . . mech-an, Mek-on . . . like that. The Mekon was meant to illustrate the depths that a scientifically based society could sink to. A specially bred super-brain with no emotions at all. All that mattered was the advance of Mekon-science.'

This was an enemy who could be easily identified, and as Frank admitted gave the readers and artists a chance to fight the Second World War all over again, with the Treens cast as the Nazis. A lot of information had by now been discovered about the scientific and medical experiments that the Germans had perpetrated in the camps with a total disregard for human life and normal moral values. This was how the Mekon behaved: he cared about nothing and no one, not even his Treens, other than advancing his own knowledge. The Mekon would return again and again, partly because he was so good at getting away, partly because the humans were too humane and would never put him to death, but mainly because he was such a strong character. He became almost as big a star as Dan in these early years, and his appearances at the numerous Hulton's Boys & Girls Exhibitions caused just as big a stir.

'Voyage to Venus' can be compared to the first album of a band. Every idea Frank, Marcus and the team ever had went into it to make it into a stunning story, taking the reader to a far-flung planet to see amazing inventions and strange new species. Some people even felt that too much was put into this first story and some of this inventiveness should have been saved for later tales. The thing with Hampson was that he was full of creativity:

> I loved inventing things for Dare, it was great fun. But I would always try to make such hardware look convincing. I found that once I began to think along certain lines all sorts of ideas would start to come to me. It was the same if I was designing a space station or a new alien life-form. We would have what we called 'ideas books' in the studio where roughs and references would be collected for use by the artists.

'Voyage to Venus' saw Dan, Digby and the team reach the far-off planet. Once there they established that it had an atmosphere that could produce food to help replace the diminishing reserves on Earth. They then had to make an alliance with the benign race who inhabited the southern hemisphere of the planet, the Therons. All this while overcoming the Mekon and his Treen forces as they tried to conquer Earth.

After seventy-seven weeks the voyage to Venus was over, the audience was ensnared and it all had to begin again. Like a pop combo whose best songs have all gone into the first album, it can be hard to then come up with something new and fresh but equally good for album number two. The time pressure was tougher in the case of Dan Dare because there was no break. As soon as the Venus adventure ended it was straight into the next story. The efforts to keep up with the weekly deadlines were taking their toll on all involved and there was little time for the team to put their heads above the parapet to look into planning the next voyage into the future. At the time they were working about six weeks in advance of publication, but that doesn't mean that when 'Voyage to Venus' ended they had a gap; they were straight into 'The Red Moon Mystery' and they had to keep the quality up.

Frank Hampson was a hard taskmaster and a perfectionist who drove himself and his team to the limits. And that was on each and every frame. Frank had overall responsibility for both the script and art on 'Voyage to Venus'. According to some sources he had advice from the esteemed science-fiction author Arthur C. Clarke for the story and obviously didn't do all the artwork himself, but the responsibility was all on his shoulders.

Many people told Frank that he had put too many of his ideas into *just* seventy-seven weeks of story. In 'Voyage to Venus' Frank invented a whole raft of new technology. The list is long and incredible so here is just some of it: personal radio, astral viewer, videophone, impulse wave engines, infrared compass, 3D television, air-intake converters, vitahypos, jepeet, helicar, paralysing pistol, space shuttle. This list comes from the first ten weeks of the Venus story. In story number two there was almost nothing left to invent. It only runs for half the number of 'episodes' and in spite of the lack of new inventions there was still much to enjoy about it and it kept the readers on board.

The original team were all there, we were introduced to the idea of space stations and living on another planet, and two much-loved characters were also introduced into the Dare universe: his uncle Dr Ivor Dare and his personal spaceship *Anastasia*.

Doctor Dare – what is it about alliteration? – was an eccentric scientist from the Welsh branch of Dan's family tree. He was on Mars researching the archaeology of the planet. His input was vital in the solving of the mystery thanks to his discoveries about the ancient civilisation ruled by Dortan-Uth-Alger. Ivor found that these previous inhabitants of Mars had been wiped out by the Red Moon. With his flash of red hair, handlebar moustache and blunt manner, he always cut straight to the chase while still having the air of a crazy scientist. A feisty, no-nonsense character, he was to return in later stories and was always welcome as he added some flavour and depth to Dan's family backstory in exactly the way Frank had intended. With his introduction the reader begins to feel that Dan has depth and breadth, and many layers which the storytellers at the *Eagle* will slowly unveil.

Over the years Dan would go on to fly many spaceships, but the one he always has closest to his heart, like your first car, was *Anastasia*. Designed by Sondar and named after Digby's aunt in gratitude for her pivotal role in thwarting the Mekon in 1996 when she picked up her nephew's hidden message, *Anastasia* was Dan's very own spaceship. At a time when many readers probably did not even have their own bicycle, the idea of owning your own spaceship must have seemed incredible.

The second tale begins with Dan and Digby on holiday, visiting Dr Dare on Mars. The year is 1999. Everyone loves the chance to peek into the private lives of the rich and famous, and fans of 'Dare' would have been no different. Once again the opening panel sells the world beautifully and creates an expectation of what is to come. While 'Voyage to Venus' began with an idealised view of what Earth's future could promise, 'The Red Moon Mystery' went further and opened with the idea of Mars as a holiday destination. And what a holiday you could have! Because of the lower gravity you could bound around the place like it was a giant playground. In that first panel a young boy is seen flying across the frame with the greatest of ease while a young lady, possibly Professor Peabody, floats by with her skis balanced delicately on one shoulder.

The holiday atmosphere is quickly dispelled with news from home and before you can say, 'What's that blazing red ball of fire heading straight for Mars?', Dare and Digby are once again on call to save the planet.

In essence the road to success was found during this first couple of years, but the stories and characters alone were not responsible for the initial and continued success of the strip and the comic. Throughout its most successful period the *Eagle* was ahead of the game in terms of finding and holding on to readers.

The launch of the comic was ground-breaking and created a lot of resentment among other publishers. Hulton used sophisticated teaser techniques to get people excited about the new arrival. Cars were sent out with enormous eagles on their roofs. These cars travelled the length and breadth of the country and were impossible to miss. This part of the campaign was described in the comic itself in a feature celebrating the first anniversary: 'At last we decided on the *Hunt the Eagle* plan. Cars with giant effigies of golden eagles on them were engaged to tour the country. Inside the cars, loudspeakers announced "*Eagle* is coming". Gift vouchers were hidden everywhere – the finder could claim a free copy at the nearest newsagent.'

Another tactic they utilised to good effect was to make sure the newsagents were not out of pocket and took no risk. For the first few weeks, Hulton encouraged newsagents to take as many copies of the comic as possible by letting them have it on a sale-or-return basis. No risk for them meant that they were prepared to order more than they may have otherwise. The competition naturally felt this was unfair. Apparently it broke an unwritten agreement against this sort of practice, but like all unwritten agreements it wasn't worth the paper it wasn't written on. The Periodical Publishers Association even managed to bring it up in the House of Commons, a few weeks after *Eagle* was launched. Harold Wilson was the President of the Board of Trade at the time and he responded to a question by a Mr Hake, who wanted to know if Wilson knew about a return to the practice of sale or return and if, in light of paper shortages, he would do anything to prevent it. Wilson drew a distinction between the practice in general and the use of it to launch new magazines for maybe a four-week period. In the latter case he was prepared to accept it. Overall he was satisfied that the good sense of the industry would prevail.* As it turned out, the whole debate was moot because there were no unsold copies to be returned.

They also had to get around the restrictions of paper rationing. Frank explained how they did it:

> There was a ruling that no new publication could come out more than once a fortnight. That's the reason for the two pages of Dare. We had two pages of everything at first and the idea that it was going to be a fortnightly thing. Then Hultons were able to get around this by taking the name of a very old paper called *Merry-Go-Round*, I think it was, and saying that *Eagle* was *Merry-Go-Round* and printing '*Merry-Go-Round*' very small in the printers' imprint in the back of the paper so it could come out once a week, which was essential to its success.

We are very used now to the clever ways of marketing men. The supermarkets have loyalty cards which tie us in, television programmes have merchandise and spin-offs which expand a programme's universe until it is all-encompassing, and the internet has become one big social network to help us keep in touch with old friends and make new ones with similar interests. In the 1950s the *Eagle* broke new ground in using all these techniques and more to ensure that it reached, and then stayed at, the top of the pile.

Loyalty schemes are now so commonplace we don't even think about them, but in the 1950s they were in

* Hansard: Periodicals (Sale or Return System), HC Deb 27 April 1950, vol. 474, c112W.

their infancy and the Eagle Club was one of the first to exploit the idea. In the first issue Marcus laid out its aims and benefits in his editor's page. It was a contract between reader and comic, with the reader having to pledge to keep up certain standards of behaviour. Eagle Club members had to agree to: enjoy life and help others do the same but not at anyone else's expense; make the best of themselves; work with others for the good of all; and always lend a hand to those in need of help. Would we join Nectar if we had to promise all this? The club aimed to link like-minded readers, to organise expeditions and holidays, and finally to make a special award to those who achieved something worthwhile.

All very worthy and exciting. By joining, which meant agreeing to the above and sending a postal order for one shilling, you received in return the Eagle Badge, a Charter of Membership and the Club Book of Rules.

The Eagle Club was an instant success. Sixty thousand joined in the first week, providing an instant cash injection of £3,000. The club not only kept readers loyal, but was another way for Marcus to expound his views on the ways we should live. As well as the all-important rules and membership book there were Eagle Club badges, ties and even a song, 'Spread Your Wings'. According to the lyrics, if you were to spread your wings 'your heart will be so gay, every day'. The club was a massive success and reached 100,000 members by the end of July 1950, and double that within three years. In fact, it became so successful that for a time in those early years they had to close the club to new members. It was spawning its own industry beyond the production of the comic and they just didn't have the staff numbers to cope.

The Eagle Club was not just a sit-at-home type of thing; it encouraged members to get out and about, specifically with the Eagle Club holidays. The aim was to give youngsters who might otherwise not get away the chance to travel and meet up with other readers. The ambitions of the club were quite amazing, with holidays going all over the world and including exotic activities such as skiing and white-water rafting. These may not seem exotic now, but this was still only the 1950s, before package holidays opened up the world. The events and trips of the Eagle Club were reported in the comic, and everyone seemed to have so much fun that it would have been most remiss not to join.

The *Eagle* was the most expensive comic on the market but still it topped the charts. With its high moral code, religious leanings and skiing holidays it is fair to say that it appealed more to middle-class readers than the other publications available. It didn't rely purely on strips and placed a high importance on educational content. In many ways, then, it was the comic for the aspirational young boy, or parent. This placed a big onus on the people behind the scenes to provide a good service to the readers, because they were more likely than readers of other comics to be inquisitive and questioning.

Rod Barzilay is known to *Eagle* fanatics as the publisher of *Spaceship Away*, a fantastic quarterly tribute to all things Dan Dare. As a lad he was a member of the Eagle Club and he still has his badge and member's card to prove it. While he never went on any of the holidays he did take up the offer of a trip to the Bertram Mills Circus. One of the things he remembers fondly is that the *Eagle* always replied to his letters. As a latecomer to the comic – he only started in 1954 – he was eager to find out what he had missed and so sent regular letters. These always got a considered response and he was even invited up to Hulton House to look through the back issues. This was something that made the *Eagle* special: this direct relationship that it had with its readers. It started of course with Marcus's column each week, in which it seemed that he was speaking directly to the reader.

Alan Vince echoes Barzilay's experiences and had ongoing correspondence with the various *Eagle* artists, including Frank Hampson. Bruce Cornwell was, during his early years, one of the staff whose job, as well as having to get the strip out every week, was replying to the queries continually coming in. Occasionally these would be printed in the letters column, but most of them would be a personal dialogue between the *Eagle* and the reader. That reader was occasionally someone from high in the British Establishment. Chad Varah recalls a letter that Marcus received from one of 'two English Royal brothers'; he doesn't say who but it is probably the princes, Edward Duke of Kent and Michael of Kent. The letter explained that at their school an instruction had been posted prohibiting comics. The royal siblings had complained to the head and shortly afterwards a postscript was added to the prohibited list stating 'except *Eagle*'.

This personal relationship with the reader was further enhanced by Hampson's insistence that all the artwork was signed:

The rates of pay that were being paid in those days for comics were very low. I had quite a job trying to convince Marcus, which I did in the end, that rather than pay £3 a page he should be paying £30. Well £30 a page in 1950 was enough for a man to live on quite comfortably, which meant he could spend the whole week doing a page. And also we could insist that he signed it. I wouldn't have unsigned work in the paper. It was one of the big bug-bears. The artist puts his reputation on the line when he signs it. Secondly, you get a personal relationship with the reader, which comes out very strongly in letters from readers. The boys used to delight in knowing that this page was done by Frank Hampson and that page was done by Frank Humphries and the other page was done by Bellamy and another page was done by Williams. One club even had a weekly stakes, who was best this week? Whereas Amalgamated Press was always completely anonymous . . . I always remember the editor's letters, they were always addressed to 'Dear chums' and they ended with 'Your editor'. There was no personal touch.

It was not just the strips that were signed. Marcus always signed his editor's page, and if he ever replied to a specific letter he did it by name.

The Eagle Carol Service was another innovation, introduced in 1951. It was the first overtly religious aspect of the comic, and it became an instant hit. The first service was held at St Paul's Cathedral, a big deal in itself, but the fact that attendees would have a service conducted by the editor of the *Eagle* was also a major point. For these readers to put a face and voice to the man

Everyone in Dan's world in one room. What could possibly go wrong? This section is comprised of more iconic moments from Dan Dare's space adventures.

A FEW MOMENTS LATER, THE TREEN CREW EMERGE FROM THE MEKON'S FLEEING FLAGSHIP . . .

WE CAN FIND NOTHING, O MASTER!

REMEMBER — DARE NEVER LIES!

YOU HAVE TWO HUNDRED SECONDS TO LIVE!

KEEP SEARCHING, FOOLS!

THE EARTHMEN STARE AT THE SCREEN IN AMAZEMENT AS THE SENSITIVE CRYPT EQUIPMENT PICKS UP IMPULSES TRANSMITTED FROM EARTH TWO-AND-A-HALF YEARS EARLIER!

...EARTH MOURNS THESE GALLANT SPACEMEN WHO PERISHED YESTERDAY IN THE SUCCESSFUL DESTRUCTION OF THE SINISTER RED MOON. CITIZENS OF THE WORLD — WE PRESENT SIR HUBERT GUEST, SPACE FLEET'S CONTROLLER!

RED MOON DESTROYED

TREEN GO... ...NOR AND COLONEL ...RE KILLED

THEY SAVED THE WORLD—TWI...

SPACEMAN DIGBY & STOWAWAY PROFESSO... PEABODY ALSO LOST IN TRAGEDY OF BOMB THAT WAS TOO GOOD

The Mekon knew that Dan's word was his bond. Unfortunately for Dan and the team, Lero was not quite so honest.

London, 2011. Digby pretends to be in charge.

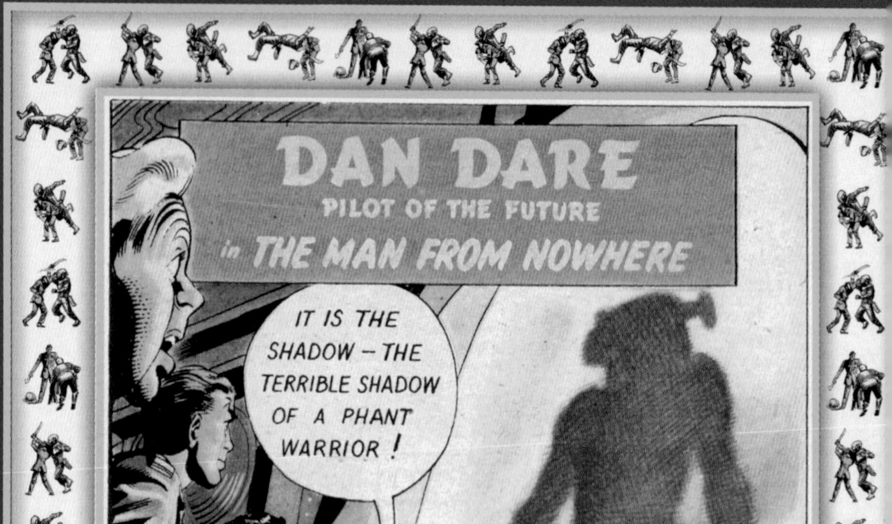
DAN DARE
PILOT OF THE FUTURE
in THE MAN FROM NOWHERE
IT IS THE SHADOW – THE TERRIBLE SHADOW OF A PHANT WARRIOR!

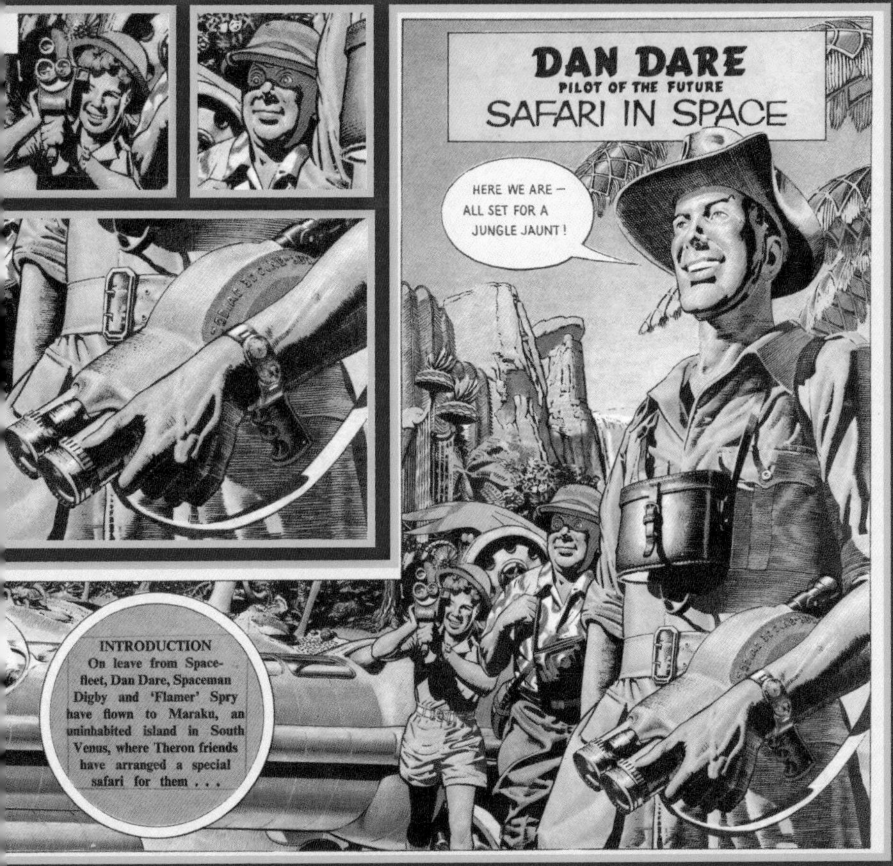
DAN DARE
PILOT OF THE FUTURE
SAFARI IN SPACE
HERE WE ARE — ALL SET FOR A JUNGLE JAUNT!
INTRODUCTION
On leave from Spacefleet, Dan Dare, Spaceman Digby and 'Flamer' Spry have flown to Maraku, an uninhabited island in South Venus, where Theron friends have arranged a special safari for them . . .

FRANK HAMPSON.
PRODUCTION

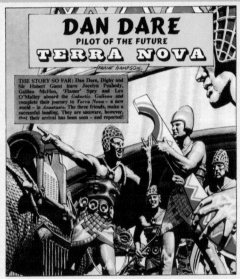

Frank Hampson's last cover was undated due to a lengthy printer's strike in the summer of 1959.

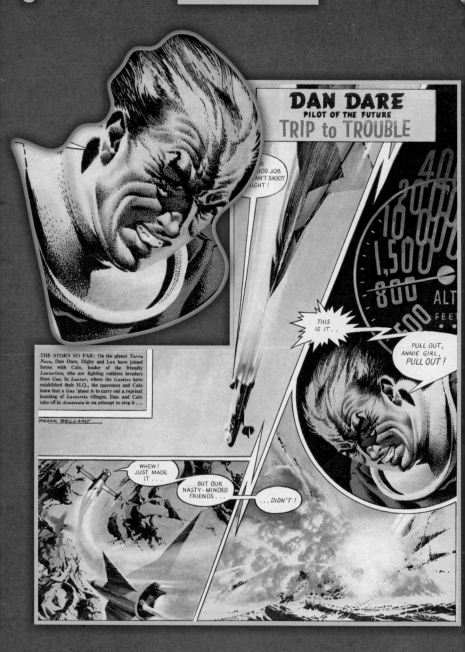

Frank Bellamy makes his mark.

behind the signature on the editor's page must have been quite something.

As well as the Eagle Club there was, of course, the merchandise. Within twelve months the first advert appeared for a Dan Dare item. The advert is in the issue dated 16 March 1951, on page 16, and offers a 'complete Dan Dare outfit'. It promises to make you the envy of all your friends with its 'smart jacket and four man-size pockets'. It comes in at 59s. 6d. with a genuine flying helmet available for a little bit extra. It really was a hard sell, with clever use of peer pressure: 'Every boy is going to want one – don't be one of those who get disappointed.' It goes on: 'Ask your dad if you can have one of the first – it's well worth it.' Fathers up and down the country must have been quickly reconsidering whether it really was a good idea to let their kids read the comic.

Before long there was not much that you could buy without it being linked to Dan Dare. There were jigsaws, board games and bagatelles. More clothes were available – you could dress head to foot as the Pilot of the Future – but the thing that sold the most were the guns. Guns of all types and sizes: rocket guns, rayguns, cosmic rayguns, even aquajet guns. The irony is not missed that one of Marcus's problems with the American comics was their unfettered violence, and yet within a couple of years of its launch *Eagle* was openly advertising all sorts of weaponry, and someone was making a hefty profit from it.

In July 1951, just over a year after *Eagle*'s launch, the Eagle Club was joined by the Horlicks Spacemen's Club, which was linked to Radio Luxembourg's broadcast of 'Dan Dare'. Appearing every weekday evening, the show

From our missionary friends overseas comes the news that EAGLE readers have responded magnificently to the suggestions we have given you from time to time to send your old copies of EAGLE to missions in various parts of the world.

The delightful picture you see here has been sent to us by the Rev Leslie F. Rooney, who is a missionary at Essequibo in British Guiana, the only British colony on the mainland of South America.

EAGLE CLUB NEWS
SAILING ON THE BROADS

The two EAGLE holiday boats, the *Olive* and the *White Moth*, with twenty *Eaglers* aboard, left Wroxham on a Sunday morning recently, to explore the Norfolk Broads for a week.

Besides being shown how to handle a sailing dinghy – an exercise which caused much amusement from time to time – the holiday included swimming, fishing, relay races and games. The weather was fairly kind and *Eaglers* finished their holiday looking bronzed and fit. We hope there will be another of these sailing holidays next year.

Above: The odd hour of leisure is taken up by feeding the swans.

Below: Keeping the deck ship-shape. There's a job for everyone aboard.

Here you see *Eaglers* on a previous winter sports holiday, being taught how to ski by an expert.

LET EAGLE TAKE YOU TO AUSTRIA

For our Winter Sports Holiday this year we have chosen the lovely centre of Steinach in Austria where, for £25 10s 0d inclusive, EAGLE readers can enjoy a really wonderful holiday for ten days, beginning on the 2nd of January.

Skiing will be taught by special instructors, and hire of skis, ski sticks, boots, etc. are all included in the charge of £25 10s 0d. The hotel accommodation is first class and there will be lashings of good food. Ask your parents if they can afford this treat for you.

For further particulars please write in, on a postcard, to EAGLE Holiday Department, 43 Shoe Lane, London E.C.4.

IT'S WIZARD!

That was the verdict of the first EAGLE readers to inspect our Exhibition of Modern Wonders. It comprises two caravans and two trailers, packed with exciting models of every kind and description.

GUESS WHERE?

They're in the Comet – BOAC's jet air-liner. After a look around this super job there's still time for reading and drawing before the kind of tea is laid on the table that is every schoolboy's dream!

EAGLE CLUB NEWS

Visit to a Sweet Factory

Twelve EAGLE Club members were recently invited to visit James Pascall's Sweet Factory, where they had a very interesting afternoon. First they saw toffee being stamped out and cut into pieces by a large metal cutter. Then they moved on to watch boiled sweets and marshmallows being made. Next visit was to the chocolate room where enormous vats of chocolate are stirred and melted and then cooked and cut into bars.

The visit ended in the factory canteen, where Pascall's kindly provided an exciting tea.

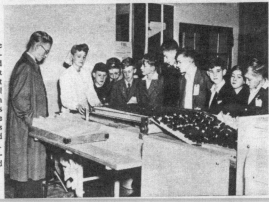

EAGLE CLUB NEWS

(Above) Coco the clown and Mr Bernard Mills chat with a party of EAGLE Club members who visited Bertram Mills Circus at Huddersfield. The circus is now rehearsing for their Christmas season and there will be a competition for you later on with a London circus visit for a prize.

(Left) The Reverend Chad Varah discusses DAN DARE with EAGLE Club members who were invited to lunch on the Hulton Press premises during September. Just behind Mr Varah is Mr Ashwell-Wood.

lasted for five years and gave birth to the club. Membership opened up a whole new world of things to buy, from Dan's cap badge and tie through to the periscope, apparently vital if you wanted to watch the Coronation parade, and even a gravityless space cup. The cup was sold as 'nearly unbreakable', but was clearly not nearly unbreakable enough as very few have survived.

On the radio Dan was played by Noel Johnson, who had found earlier fame playing the earthbound special agent Dick Barton. The stories that made up the serial were new and separate from those in the comic. Sadly no record of them exists and it has become something of a fool's quest trying to find them. According to all sources, they were recorded on vinyl at the Star Sound studios in London. These discs were played on air and then destroyed. For Dare fans the discs have become something of a holy grail. A rumour was doing the rounds that there are copies in Spain, but so far nothing has been found. Along with an original drawing of Dan as Lex Christian, this is the thing aficionados would most like to find in someone's attic.

Having ruled the roost in the UK for a year, Marcus was keen to see what Dan could do overseas. While Dan Dare was a particularly – peculiarly, even – British character, that did not stop him trying his hand in many markets. In some instances this was as a full *Eagle* reprint on foreign soil, but in others it involved Dan being adopted by a local comic and put in among the normal features.

The first foreign foray was to that old outpost of the British Empire, Australia, where Issue 1 was produced on 21 May 1953. The staff back home would have been happy to see it titled *Eagle Magazine*, as they always felt slightly put down by it being called a 'comic'.

For eighty-six weeks, Australian children were given a rerun of what British readers had seen three years previously. Obviously the letters pages and other specifically British content were changed, but other than that it was pretty much the same. Initially sales peaked in the mid-70,000s, but when they slumped to the low tens of thousands, the end was nigh. The death knell was sounded by the British version itself being imported into the country. Before Australian publication finished on 27 January 1955 it was helpfully suggested that readers take up the British edition. However, no advice was offered on how to catch up on what had happened to the story in between the adventures the Australians had been reading and the ones in the British version – although the final issue did give a brief summation of all the plots that were partly completed.

When *Eagle* appeared briefly in Sweden, its name was changed to *Falken* and Dan became Dan Djärv Framtidspilot, which translates as Dan Bold, Future Pilot. As in Australia, this was an attempt to transplant the whole comic to the new country with as few changes as possible for the locals. Only two other regulars had to change their names: Professor Brittain became Professor Puff, while Harris Tweed was renamed Harry Ullman.

Sweden jumped straight into 'Prisoners of Space' ('Fängar I Rymden'), but sadly the country was not smitten with *Falken* and it ceased publication after just eighteen weeks. Neighbouring Norway tried a similar tack with *Hauk*, again opening with 'Prisoners of Space'. (A unique aspect of this publication was that it was in landscape format.) *Hauk* began with a freebie in 1955, followed by four further issues that year. The publishing plan seemed designed to ensure that no one could have followed it, as it was neither monthly nor weekly; around thirty issues were produced for each of the following two years. Finland also got in on the act, but not until the 1960s, when the Keith Watson-drawn story 'Operation Time Trap' was run as 'Operaatio ajanmurtaja' in the comic *Nastasarjat* (which translates as *Pin Sets* in English).

Eagle then hit the news-stands in the Netherlands in October 1955 under the name *Arend*. This was one of the most successful and longest-running of the foreign *Eagle*s, and ran until 1966. It even copied the club, and included strips from the other Hulton comics *Swift* and *Girl*. Digby became Dirk Vis – maybe they felt he was a fish out of water – while Peabody was Meeuwes (sadly no humorous translation there).

It was never very likely that such a typical Brit as Dan would do so well in France, but *Dan Dair* was published by Editions Lug for one year from April 1962. This monthly series covered three adventures: 'Voyage to Venus', 'The Red Moon Mystery' and 'Marooned on Mercury'.

Dan's first appearance in a foreign language, however, was in Italy, when he turned up in *Disco Volante* (*Flying Saucer*). It was a faithful reproduction of *Eagle* which only lasted ten weeks and began with, but obviously never ended, the Venus story. Maybe it was jinxed when the eagle was replaced in the red masthead by a flying saucer. Dan had more success in Italy when *Il Giorno dei Ragazzi* brought him on board in March 1957, beginning with 'Rogue Planet'. This comic was a freebie given away each week inside the national daily *Il Giorno*, which had first been published in 1956. *Girono dei Regazzi* continued, along with Dan, for over eleven years. Italy also got to see Dan sporadically in *L'Avventuroso* during the 1970s.

In Portugal Dan appeared in *Titã* (*Titan*), on the front cover of its twenty-fifth issue. As with many of the comics on the continent, *Titã* did not last long enough to see the resolution to the tale and disappeared in less than a year, after only forty-seven issues. Dan subsequently appeared in two other short-lived comics, *O Falcão* (*The Hawk*) and *Foguetão* (*Rocket*), although in the latter he was now called Capitao Marte (Captain Mars) and the story was 'O Planeta Desconhecido' ('The Unknown Planet'), which we know as 'Terra Nova'. What they thought of the Hampson-to-Bellamy changeover is anyone's guess, but at least they saw some classic examples of both their work.

Yugoslavian publisher Vjesnik licensed Dan for *Plavi Vjesnik* (*Blue Herald*), renaming him Den Deri – Pilot Buducnosti, and he served them well from 1954 to 1973. This magazine succeeded by cleverly combining a strong selection of excellent foreign-sourced material and exciting work from local artists.

The success of the *Eagle* and Dan abroad rested on two main factors. In Holland the magazine succeeded because the Dutch and the English are quite similar as people. There were also the warm feelings that the Dutch had towards the British, who had helped to rid them of German rule: Dan was as much a symbol of a wartime hero as he was over here. In less Anglophile countries the comic succeeded most when its elements were combined with local ingredients, as in Italy and Yugoslavia. Where Dan and other contents of the *Eagle* were simply transplanted into foreign soil without support, they generally failed.

And so by the mid-1950s Dan Dare and his crew were dominating the airwaves, the newsagents' shelves, the toy shops and pretty much everything in the lives of children the length and breadth of this and many other countries. When asked why he thought the *Eagle* was so successful, Frank had a few theories.

I think it expressed pretty well what boys at that time were hunting; it was optimistic. It came at a time of great shortages after a very long and exhausting war, when everything was very bare, everything was 'utility', everything was right down to rock bottom, and so the fantasy in it had an appeal, the colour in it had a very great appeal. Generally it expressed the ideals of the time, which were based on the United Nations organisation. We thought it was a brave new world: UNO was going to run everything, there was going to be a world government. Although the bright ideas everybody always has when they're young and idealistic seem on the point of coming true, they didn't, of course, but I think to great extent they [the stories] expressed that feeling. And of adventure, of course.

He went on:

> We took them seriously, you can't tell now from looking
> at these how novel they were when they came out. Sec-
> ondly there was the big picture on the right of the *Eagle*
> rectangle each week, which I was careful to vary as much
> as I could between humour, drama and novelty. In the
> third place the fact that we drew most of the figures
> from life . . . made them much more convincing. And the
> stories were good I think.

He paused at this point and looked briefly at his hands
and then at the interviewer, and finished with a chuckle:
'My genius, of course.' He was only half joking.

Terry Jones sums it up:

> 'It was such an amazing thing of its time, it was part of
> the post-war waking-up world, sort of opening of hori-
> zons, opening them for children and getting away from
> the restriction of the past, the establishment saying,
> "Comics are disgraceful and disgusting and you shouldn't
> read them." And actually saying there's nothing wrong
> with the form.'

All this magic had sprung from the imagination of Frank
Hampson, the determination of Marcus Morris and the
risk-taking of Hulton Press, and was to continue into
the late 1960s after all three of these parties had departed
the scene. If the strength of something can be counted
by how long it lasts after its creator has moved on, then
Dan Dare was certainly something special.

CHAPTER FOUR

Frank Hampson's Studio System

THERE IS A photograph of Frank Hampson that shows him leaning over his work, pipe poking out from his mouth, his head in a cloud of smoke, as the sun sets outside and day turns to evening. He was meticulous and worked himself to a standstill in his search for perfection. It is clear that when Hampson was at the helm the quality of 'Dan Dare' was at its peak, but he couldn't do it by himself. As the leader of the Dan Dare team, he drove the artists in his employ as hard as he did himself. But although it was a team effort – a bit like the Hollywood 'studio system' in the 1920s and 1930s* – Frank's inability to fully let go led to him making himself ill. (It is also the case that because 'Dan Dare' was so much Frank's vision, when he did finally depart the scene it was never quite the same, and neither was Frank.)

The studio system ran pretty much from before the first

---

* A means of production and distribution whereby large movie studios produced films primarily on their own lots with creative personnel under often long-term contract.

issue of the *Eagle* for almost ten years, and created some of the most memorable comic-strip work this country, and the world, has ever seen. There is no reason to think that they could not have continued for many years: standards had not dropped; in fact they were getting better and better. But in 1959 Hulton Press was sold to Odhams Press and changes were introduced. Sometimes change is just for change's sake, but in this case it was driven by cost-cutting. The studio system was an enormously expensive way to create two pages of a boys' comic – but quality does not come cheap. The thinking was that if some money could be saved, and the quality only marginally cut, then everyone would be happy. If only life were so easy.

The team that Hampson built around him was a mixture of enthusiastic novices in their first job and others with real experience. There was a strong range of skills, and a desire to produce something special. They were in the main artists or colourists, but there was one who had no experience or training in any of this. He wasn't an artist or a writer but over time he became as important as any of them. To readers of 'Dan Dare' all over the country he was instantly recognisable as Sir Hubert Guest, Controller of Space Fleet; to Frank he was Dad; and to the rest of the team he was known as Pop.

Robert Hampson, retired from the police force, filled many roles, but one of his most important was that of team glue. Stationed, but never sitting down, at his high desk in the corner of The Bakery, 22 Botanic Road, Southport, he held the team together with his good humour and his tea-making duties, which he mainly shared with Joan Porter. All of the team speak of him with genuine heartfelt warmth. Greta Tomlinson remembers him as 'a super chap. I really liked him. Not quite sure exactly what he did but he always seemed to be busy. He did errands, looked things up for us, did the post.' Joan Porter has a clearer memory of what Robert did, '[he] worked wonders as secretary, model, provider of second-hand furniture, useful articles and constant firm cheerfulness'. Robert's daughter Margaret is obviously biased, but she recalled, 'Dad was great. Everybody liked him. I can't think of anyone that would say a bad word about him. They really liked him at the *Eagle*.' It is ironic that the man who held the lowliest position in the team – unofficially he was the tea boy – was the model for the top dog at Space Fleet.

After Robert, the member of the team whom Frank had known the longest was Harold Johns, a quiet, some would say shy, artist born in Somerset. He and Frank had met as students at Victoria College in 1938. When war came and they both went off to fight, Johns was in the Yorkshire Hussars, for whom he drove tanks. While in the forces he trained as a cartographer and was even awarded the British Empire Medal. They kept in touch sporadically during the conflict and when it was over they both returned and enrolled at the Southport School of Arts and Crafts. While honing their skills on the course they used their spare time to try and get commercial work. When Marcus Morris came a-calling it was natural that Frank would bring his old mate along. Harold was in a way the third Eagle, if we can call him that. He was there from the very start, helping Frank with both the original dummy that Marcus would take to London and the later one. His signature appears in this second dummy, as the artist for a 'Sporting Personalities' profile of the Hull City inside-forward Raich Carter.

Jocelyn Thomas's first job as an artist was on *The Anvil*, as illustrator for a piece entitled 'The Church Clock'. In fact, a lot of future *Eagle* artists crop up in the *Anvil*s of mid- to late 1949, including Norman Thelwell (who would go on to create 'Chicko' for the comic but is best known now for his humorous cartoons of ponies) and John Ryan, best known now for *Captain Pugwash*. Pugwash did appear in early *Eagle* issues, but was dumped by Marcus Morris for being too juvenile. Ryan came back with his ever popular and long-lasting Harris Tweed character. Jocelyn, though, was only with the *Eagle* for two years, as a colourist. It was thanks indirectly to the *Eagle* that she found her husband, which in turn led to her departure. When the team moved south, some of them stayed at the Linden House Hotel and it was another guest here whom she married and moved to India with.

The *Eagle* studio was unusual for the times in that it employed three women. The other two were Greta Tomlinson and Joan Porter. The *Dictionary of British Comic Artists, Writers and Editors* gives Porter a rather cursory entry, as secretary, researcher and photographer, and you would not know from this that she was taken on as an artist, working mainly on colouring. She later received a letter from Hampson in which he wrote, 'Wherever I am and whatever I am working on I shall want you for the colour.' Tomlinson came from the grandest art background, as a graduate of the Slade School of Fine Art. She started there in 1944, when it was moved to Oxford during the war, and finished in 1949. While her training covered all aspects of fine art, she specialised in figures and it was for this that Frank initially hired her. Although a native of Burnley, she was eager to stay in London after graduating and took her portfolio around the various studios and fashion houses before responding to an advert in the *Advertisers Journal*. The advert didn't say it was for the *Eagle*: in the development days everything was topsecret, as Hulton didn't want the competition finding out what it was doing. Tomlinson recalls accepting the job without even knowing who she was going to be employed by. To give herself a better chance of being interviewed she said that she was soon to be coming up north on a trip home.

Frank did all the interviewing, but it was his work that convinced Greta, rather than anything he said. 'Frank's work was on the board and I just thought it was stunning, I mean absolutely stunning, and I thought, I've got to get this job.' After the interview she was offered the job on a starting pay of £4. 10s.

Frank's baker's half-dozen was completed by Eric Eden and Bruce Cornwell. Born in the West Country in 1924, Eric was a land worker during the war before he too, like Frank and Harold, turned up at the Southport School of Art. They knew him from there, and trusted that with a similar training to them he would be up to the task. Joan Porter refers to Eden as the 'king of the airbrush' as this was an area where he ruled supreme over everyone, even Frank. (According to Frank the recruitment process was tough because there just weren't that many artists around who could produce the standard of work he required.)

If Eden was a known quantity, Canadian-born, USA-raised, motorbike-riding Cornwell was anything but. In England he trained at the Regent Street Polytechnic, which at the time was world-renowned as a blueprint for applied education. From there he went on to another world-famous institution, the Académie Julian in Paris. Like all the artists on the comic, his life was interrupted by the war. As a Canadian he was not able to join the Allied forces, and so he joined the Merchant Navy, transporting vital supplies through dangerous waters.

At the time he saw the advert for the *Eagle*, he was doing general illustration and technical drawing work, mainly for women's magazines, engineering publications and galleries, and was well established in the field. His work had slackened off a little and so he sent off for the application form. When it arrived, however, Cornwell was unimpressed and binned it, only to receive a terse phone call from Marcus Morris asking him why he hadn't replied. He reconsidered, had an interview, and Frank was sufficiently impressed to offer him the job, which was initially to be specifically on technical parts of the strip such as the buildings, the machinery and, of course, the spaceships.

This was the artistic team – some would say the whole team – but there are claims that there was a further member of the team, one whom none of them ever met. The first thing that people think of when they hear the

The creators and the star: Dan with Frank Hampson and Marcus Morris, as drawn by Don Harley. Frank and Marcus with their wives Dorothy and Jessica.

Michael (surname
unknown) the
original Flamer Spry

Ronald Graham, posing
as Dom Pierre, later the
model for Uncle Hoo.

Robert M Hampson
Frankie's Father

Robert Mason Hampson

Eric Eden as
Lex O'Malley

Don Harley 1961
age 34

Frank Hampson & Eric Eden

Bruce Cornwell as
Blasco, 1953.

Keith Watson
1957 or 8

Don Harley as Digby

Max Dunlop
as Friday

Max as
Dan Dare

Robert 'Pop' Hampson would never know what the day promised.

no helmet

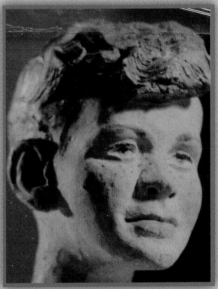

Greta Tomlinson, Eric Eden, Bruce Cornwell (helmeted) and Don Harley, Flamer Spry.

Models were vital in the studio's work.

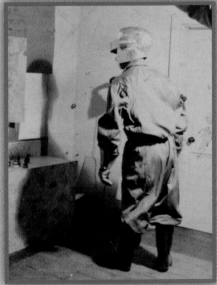

Human models were also vital in the studio's work. Note the concentric circles on the floor, which were important for scale.

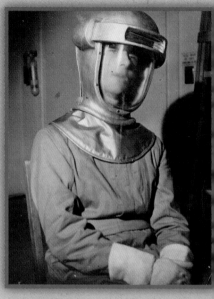

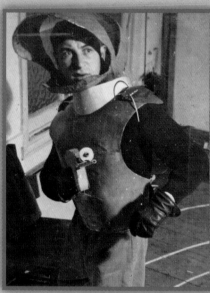

Another day at the office for Bruce Cornwell and (bottom right) Don Harley.

name 'Arthur C. Clarke' is probably *2001: A Space Odyssey*. Clarke was born almost exactly a year before Frank Hampson and had not been writing science fiction for long when, it is claimed, he was commissioned to help out on the first story for 'Dan Dare'. Frank Hampson has suggested that Clarke came up with the Treens, but others who worked on 'Dan Dare' disagree and can't remember any involvement from him at all. In Neil McAleer's 450-page biography of Clarke, *Odyssey*, there are just two sentences that mention his involvement. One suggests that he was 'science and plot adviser'; the other, in relation to the death of Marcus Morris, states in passing that he gave technical and plot advice when problems occurred.

Sixty years later his contribution, or lack of it, is still the subject of an ongoing debate among *Eagle* watchers. At one extreme he is recorded as saying that he had no involvement at all, and at the other he himself claimed to have created the Treens, and heavily influenced the plot of 'Voyage to Venus'. The evidence is murky and it seems the truth may never be established. What is not in doubt is that Clarke used a couple of pen names, one of which was Charles Willis, and it was under this name that he had a short 'story of the future' published in the *Eagle* on 4 August 1950. He also contributed an article to the 1953 *Dan Dare Space Book*.

With or without Clarke, Frank had now got his team together, and they set about getting the 'Dan Dare adventure' in motion. But Frank did not put his strip together like anyone had ever done before.

Dan Dare was painstakingly researched and realised,

and the starting point for each frame was always the characters. Each one was based on photographic reference material, usually using studio members to pose as the characters. Photographs would be taken of the 'models'' faces from every possible angle, giving perfect reference for whatever action might occur.

Frank's son Peter was only three when the *Eagle* started, and he would become the model for Flamer Spry. He recalls the photography sessions becoming a normal part of his life:

> When it all came together in Bayford Lodge we lived upstairs and the studio was downstairs and so I was always knocking around. The first time I appeared in the strip was in the Venus story as a sort of three- or four-year-old. [I was] quite recognisable as just a kid in the script. I recall posing as Flamer pretty much because I was the right sort of size and shape. Visually it wasn't particularly taken from me. We used to have loads of photos taken in the studio, which have all now gone, but there were loads of me in my kit with my Flamer Spry hat and rifle and all the rest of it, so I was quite used to posing. By then it was part of everyday life. It was what every now and then you did, along with everyone else.

The kid in the Venus story to whom Peter is referring is the Theron child who appears in Issue 36 aboard President Kalon's floating house in the scene where Dan is pleading for them to sacrifice their easy life to help others.

Frank continued to use this method after he left 'Dan

Dare' and was working with just Joan Porter on 'The Road of Courage', which recreated the life of Jesus in comic-strip form and was his last work for the *Eagle*. Peter remembers: 'Quite a few of my schoolmates from secondary school, first and second year, are there in "Road of Courage" as characters, young kids when Jesus was a boy. Everyone got roped in.'

This was not how it was originally meant to be, however. When Greta Tomlinson was first hired Frank had hoped that she would draw the figures and he would then work on these to produce the characters. It didn't work because, as she herself says, she was petrified and it just took too long. So it was decided that photographs would be best and it was this method that gave all the characters a reality that other strips just didn't have.

As an interesting aside, when Frank Bellamy went to work on 'Thunderbirds' in *TV21* he couldn't bring himself to draw them as the puppets they were on screen.* Thus when you look at his versions they seem like real people, much more real than they were ever meant to be. And so it was in 'Dan Dare', since most of the main characters were based wholly or partly on real people. Dan himself was based on Frank, but the Frank that he really wanted to be. The trademark wiggle in the eyebrows, which he also incorporated into his signature, was inspired by a scar of Frank's, caused by a bang to the head while driving his truck in the war.

---

* *TV21*, first published in 1965 as *TV Century 21*, was the comic produced to showcase the various Gerry Anderson television series such as *Thunderbirds*, *Fireball XL5*, *Captain Scarlet* and *Stingray*. Bellamy was only one of many ex-*Eagle* artists to make the switch.

If Dan was how Frank wanted to be, then Digby was closer to how he really saw himself, although he seems to be a mix of influences. Other members of the studio felt he was physically based on Harold Johns, and Frank has stated that he was 'a combination of myself and a batman I had in the army – a chap called Thornton. He wasn't Dig's build but had that type of outlook and attitude to life.' Guest was Pop: 'He became the most lifelike of all my creations. It was just a question of drawing a series of pictures of a real person.' Professor Peabody was Greta Tomlinson, but was given the name Jocelyn so that Jo Thomas was included.

Frank wasn't satisfied with just taking pictures of his staff in their civvies. We all know how wearing different clothes affects the way we stand, walk and behave. The actor Sir John Gielgud, for instance, would always begin his characterisations by finding the right pair of shoes. The models had to be wearing the right clothes and so, quite naturally, costumes were made.

It was important to Frank that the characters were all easily identifiable and distinct – hence the gimmick of Dan's eyebrows. 'Likewise I gave Digby very simplified eyes, just round circles. I think the main crew were all easily recognisable [even] when kitted out in bulky space suits. And I was able to show them all in one frame and didn't need a caption to say who was who.'

Frank made a distinction between characters based on real people, such as Guest and Peabody, and those he conjured out of thin air, such as Lex O'Malley. O'Malley joined Dan's crew in 'The Man from Nowhere'. He is seen in the first frame, which depicts the Venusian

Embassy party. He is talking to President Kalon when Dan spots him across the crowded room and asks Guest, 'Who's the naval type sporting the black beard?' Guest introduces him as 'the Great Submarine explorer'. And so, in just two frames, he has been well established: the black beard lets us know there is a little devilment in him, and the fact that Dan spots him among so many other guests indicates he has something special about him. So when the alarm at Space Fleet HQ interrupts the party, it is not surprising that, in spite of not being a space pilot, he tags along with Dan and Digby. Hampson refers to his creation of O'Malley as a 'mind-drawing'. 'He was pure fiction but a character I liked a lot. It helps if you draw a "type" if you feel a kind of fondness for them.'

The fact that O'Malley was a 'mind-drawing' doesn't seem to make him any less well realised in the strip. If you look at any of the single-frame portraits of him, it almost seems that Hampson was trying to compensate for the fact that he was not based on a real person by making him look more real than those who were.

Hampson produced a reference drawing of all the main characters, somewhat in the style of a police station identity line-up. This showed everybody's height and build so that they could be easily compared and contrasted, and ensured they always stayed the same relative to each other. Thus, whichever artist was doing a frame they would be able to ensure that Digby was always the same height relative to Dan, or Sondar, and so on. As well as photo references, they also made plaster models of all the main characters' heads. The beauty of this method was that it was so much easier for the artist to visualise a scene, or to see a character from any angle.

This sort of process was also applied to the buildings, the spacecraft and even the landscapes where these characters existed and came to life. Models were built of everything and anything, and miniatures of all the characters were used to set the scene.

One of Frank's technical obsessions was making sure that the source of the light in any frame was established. As a trained artist with a strong eye for realism, Frank was extremely concerned with light and the source of it. When you look at any frame from the comic during these years you will always be able to tell where the light that illuminates the scene is coming from. It is the light that gives each picture its depth. This in turn meant that it was easier to get the scaling and perspective right. It also meant that continuity was maintained from frame to frame, strip to strip, story to story, across the years. It would perhaps have been excusable to expend all this energy on the large opening frame next to the masthead, the shop window so to speak, but all this detail, research and effort went into every single frame.

Frank explained how the whole process came together:

The words and the pictures were worked out together each week. We worked on a three-week basis. If you take the second week of the three weeks, I would be designing the rough, the layout, the visualisation for the next week, and also doing the finished pictures which I had allotted to myself for that week, while the others were doing the other pictures.

The roughs would be given to Joan Porter and she would take figure photos and collect all the necessary reference from whatever source for that page so that when the third week came around on my desk would come the rough and all the necessary material to draw the pages and I would simply allot parts of it to Don or Eric.

There was the difficulty that when you had finished an instalment it went off and you didn't see it again for five weeks because it took that length of time to do the colour printing. Which meant that to keep things absolutely exact and accurate you either had to have voluminous notes or you had to make models, which was the favourite way. This was the best way: if you were using several people, and don't want to tie them down to copying or imitating your style, you'd give them the same to draw; and their style may vary a bit but it would still be recognisable.

As he rather modestly said of the whole process: 'When it worked it was good.'

There were usually nineteen or twenty frames in each two-page episode, and so, while the process produced brilliant results, it was time-consuming, exhausting and expensive work. There were no digital cameras of course: everything was done by hand, and materials were still at a premium. To save time, all the developing and printing was done in-house, but this took one or two artists away from their boards for a good length of time. The hours that the team had to work would not get past European Union regulations today! The trade unions would be up in arms and consequently the comic would never be made. Even Frank acknowledged this: 'I doubt if it could be done, or tolerated . . . it's all much more professional now. We were in at the beginning.' To a man, and woman, one of the main things they all mention is the torturously long hours.

Greta Tomlinson has looked back at her diaries from |the period and quotes the following typical entries: 'Worked till 3 a.m.', 'Worked till 5 a.m.', 'Worked till 4 a.m.', and one of them, which made me laugh, was 'Worked till 3 a.m., Frank gave me the rest of the day off'. She wasn't sure if that meant the rest of the day she had just finished, or the rest of the day that was about to start, but it was most likely the former. She goes on to say, 'I remember being so exhausted that I began to see in black and white, that I always remember. You were so conscious of the creases in a shirt, or how did this go or how did that go, [and] how to reproduce it. Obviously I was going a bit potty.' In fact, she started having hallucinations and losing her train of thought halfway through a sentence.

Don Harley's recollections are not dissimilar.

I can't remember having a bank holiday off in the whole time Frank was there. I always used to come in late, about ten o'clock, and Frank would tell me that I'd get more done if I came in on time, but I work better later in the day and we'd always be there late anyway. If I went home at five or six and Frank saw me leaving he would normally ask what time I was coming back, and he didn't mean the next day. He even sent me telegrams in the early evening suggesting I come back to work.

There is a picture taken by Harley in the late 1950s showing Keith Watson asleep on his drawing board. Apparently Marcus Morris chose this moment to pop in for a very rare visit and Harley remembers the reverend not looking particularly impressed by what he saw. 'I don't think he had a very high opinion of artists.'

But staff falling asleep at their desks was not unusual. Part of the problem was that Frank was continually coming up with new and better ideas. A regular occurrence was that Frank would prepare visuals (quickly prepared rough drawings of each panel), they would do the photography based on them and the frames would be allocated to the artists. They would start work and be on the verge of finishing when Frank would come back with a better idea and new visuals, and they had to start all over again. The problem was that he never, literally never, stopped working.

Bruce Cornwell realised very soon after arriving at The Bakery, or Bakehouse as he calls it (it's a Canadian thing), that the amount of work required would never fit into a normal forty-hour week. He tried to talk to Frank about the method of working, but to no avail. Everything had been fine initially but, says Cornwell, who is now in his eighties, 'the problems started when the publication date was brought forward'. This was done because Hulton were convinced that the Express group were planning to beat them to the news-stand with a new comic of their own. It came to nought in the end but it had the result of ramping up the pressure on the Bakery boys, and girls.

One of the other main reasons their workload was so

high was because of 'Dare' being two pages long. We've seen how the comic went from a planned fortnightly production to a weekly one, but this had a knock-on effect. Frank explained that, when the plan changed for it to be a weekly:

> They liked the look of the two pages on the front so much that they said, although we cut everything else down to one page, 'Dare' must stay at two pages. Which meant that I was lumbered with a lot more work than I was capable of. But in the event it became a very interesting thing to try and use people to the best advantage on the strip. And we worked out a system of doing so. To me it gave us another advantage in that we were not limited to what one man could do in a week.

So Frank remembers it as a positive, but Cornwell disagrees:

> Frank was upset by all the pressure that was on him and began to look at me and say, 'I don't like this, you got that wrong.' I stood up for myself because technically I knew where I was and I wasn't making any mistakes. So in the end he got so fed up with this that he said, 'Well, you better go back to London.' In other words I was sacked. Which was fine by me; at that stage it was murderous. Working over a hundred hours a week was no fun.

Cornwell left during 'Voyage to Venus' but the rest of the team held firm.

Another artist who passed through while Dan was battling it out on Venus was Terry Maloney. He had left his studies at Richmond Art School to join the International Brigades in the Spanish Civil War. From that conflict he went straight into the Second World War, after which he worked as a commercial artist before joining the *Eagle* team in 1950. He'd fought the Fascists in two wars and he fought to change Frank Hampson's work methods, but this was a battle he lost. After his brief time at the *Eagle* – he was only there for a few months – he became well known as an amateur astronomer.

Cornwell and Maloney were the exceptions, though, because in those early days the team enjoyed each other's company and realised very early on that they were involved in something beyond anything that had been done before. Tomlinson recalls, 'It became like a family in the end, and we were all half dead anyway with tiredness, and the radio was on nearly all the time. The song at the time was "Bewitched, Bothered and Bewildered", and that seemed to suit us very well. It was a very happy atmosphere and we had a lot of laughs. For some reason, we all started to speak in a Lancashire accent.'

If Pop Hampson was the binding force that held the team together, Frank was the driving force that kept them moving forward. He led from the front and was always the first to arrive and the last to leave. Tellingly, none of them seems to remember ever seeing Frank draw his visuals, implying that he did them after they'd gone home: further proof that he worked as hard, if not harder than the team. When you have a boss like that it is much harder to slacken off yourself. Frank had high standards, which he expected everyone to live up to, but he was just as hard on himself. It is tempting to imagine that he would be working within the team, but he was very much the leader and kept himself quite separate. He was ten years older than many of the members and had a strong authority over them. This is illustrated by the fact that Greta did not realise for some time that Harold and Frank had been at art school together and were old friends. 'There didn't seem to be that camaraderie between them that you'd expect [from old schoolmates]. Harold was just another member of the team.'

The studio worked very much as a factory would, with the artists on an assembly line, just part of the process with no real view of the bigger picture. So they had little idea of where the story was going and what was happening on it from week to week, and certainly none of them had any input in the story. Throughout his time with 'Dan Dare' Frank was the person in charge of the plots and scripts but he fell into this rather by accident.

At first I had no thought of doing the script. In the first place I simply designed and drew three dummy issues of the whole paper so that Marcus would have something in his hand to sell when he went looking for finance.

A script writer came in, Guy Morgan; he lasted about five instalments, and then sent for me halfway through a week. He gave me a nice lunch and then said he'd no idea how to proceed, claiming that he'd had a classical education that didn't fit him for inventing things. My estimate had always been that one man could do one page in a week, to attain the kind of standard that I hoped we'd get. So it was case of grabbing my art student friends from the Southport School of Art and hiring The Bake-house and get cracking and just keep the thing going as best we could. This is how I came to write the story.

He didn't write them all. Alan Stranks did that, from 'Operation Saturn' all the way through to 'Safari in Space', a period that began in February 1953 and went through to May 1959, but Frank worked with him on the story arcs. The only time he totally vacated this role was when Chad Varah took over for 'Marooned on Mercury' while Frank rested under doctor's orders.

Research into the behaviour and attitudes of factory workers during the 1960s identified the workforce's dis-sociation from their employers because of their lack of involvement in the overall process. This was obviously equally true of the artists working on 'Dan Dare', as Don Harley remembers: 'This chap asked me if I enjoyed my time on *Eagle*. When I replied that it was just a job his jaw almost hit the floor. He couldn't believe that I had worked with *the* Frank Hampson and just called it a job.'

The artwork obviously took up vast amounts of time, but it was all based on the scripts; these had to be the starting point. As we've already seen, the Venus story was almost exclusively Frank's work, with some possible input from Arthur C. Clarke. While Frank has admitted that the art took a while to find its own style – it began with too much of an American influence – the scripts were strong from day one. The first problem that faces any writer is the main plot: 'What story am I going to tell?' With 'Voyage to Venus' this could be summed up as 'The Earth is running out of food, and the inhabitants go to Venus to find a replacement source.' Much of the flesh on those bones came from Frank's army experience:

> The uniforms actually were my uniform, just painted green instead of khaki. The general atmosphere in particular of the service involved was simply those of the British Army. The relationships between officer, batman, private, that sort of thing, which I knew because I'd been in the army for six and a half years. The dialogue was almost second nature. All that remained to do was to invent what happened when you got wherever you were going.

He makes it seem quite straightforward, but he's being modest. The problem faced by a comic-strip writer is that each week has to end on a cliffhanger. This in turn means that each week has to begin with a resolution to last week's cliffhanger. In the middle you have to move the story forward. We know how short time was for the artwork, and it was equally so for the scripts. While the overall story arc was in place early on, the mini-climaxes and resolution were worked out on the way and room was allowed for minor tangents.

Overall, 'Venus' works well as we move from the initial crisis of the *Kingfisher* exploding. A solution is found, by Dan of course, and then we're on Venus. The introduction of obstacles throughout ramps up the tension: first, the radio almost destroying Dan and Digby's ship, then the dangers of the Flamebelt, and finally the discovery that not everyone on Venus is friendly. This gives a lot for the crew to deal with and allows the story to meander a little while still focusing on the final goal: food. This goal gives rise to one of the classic frames, of Guest leaning back in the verdant Venus jungle and dreaming of 'pheasant with all the trimmings'. This leads each crew member to think of their favourite meal: Dan wants 'steak, fried onions and potatoes'; Digby would be happy with 'a fish and sixpennyworth with plenty of salt and vinegar'. As these three dream, the practical Peabody has collected a veritable feast from the jungle they are sitting in. The whole scene reminds us neatly why they are on this crazy trip, tells us a little about each of them, and emphasises once more the intelligence and practical nature of the Prof. The script-writing balancing act is kept up all the way through the first story; the pace never lags and reading it now, in collected form, it is a classic page-turner: you want to know what happens next, how they get out of each scrape. It is this that made people buy it each week.

These first few months were all spent in The Bakery, which was rented for the team to work in but never really suited them. It's still there today and has hardly changed at all. It was damp and cold, and the lighting was far from perfect. The old oven was still in the corner, as if to remind everyone that it was a bakery, not an artists' studio. Cornwell describes it as an 'overcrowded hell-hole', but also recalls that there was 'never any friction with anyone' (maybe he forgets his odd argument with Frank), though he agrees with Tomlinson that they never really socialised: 'There was never any time.'

Things had got so cramped that, in the month or so before he left, Cornwell was booted out to a room above a pub, where he had none of the reference material needed to do the job properly. This made life impossible and was probably an additional factor in his departure from the team and his move back to London. He didn't know it then but, just as the Mekon was chasing Dan Dare all over Venus, the rest of the team were not far behind him. With the long hours and The Bakery proving inadequate, moves were afoot to shift the team to a more suitable location, nearer to Hulton HQ.

And so, late in 1950, the big move south took place. As can be imagined, it was quite an upheaval for everyone involved. Greta Tomlinson remembers everyone living in hotels and guesthouses: 'At the end of the year we were moved down to Epsom, which was very nice. I lived in a hotel, Linden House [now an old people's home], which was on the same road as The Firs, the Morris residence and also our new workplace. Joan lived in a guesthouse just nearby, Harold was in an annexe of the hotel, and I shared a room with Jocelyn.'

The only major addition to the team down in Surrey was Don Harley. He was a student at the nearby Epsom College of Art when he first met Frank, who had come to the college to give a talk about the *Eagle* and 'Dan Dare'. The students there rather looked down on the comic-strip artist and his tales of rockets but Don, who had trained under Sir Stanley Spencer, was won over and applied for a job at the nearby studio.

As Greta explained above, the new 'studio' was part of the Morris family's new home. With the expense required to move so many people the length of the country, you might expect that new workspace to be chosen with great care. But, as for Digby travelling through a telesender, life is not always as we expect or hope. The Firs was a very pleasant family home, set in beautiful grounds, but it was not the fully equipped studio that had been promised, and it meant sharing space with Jessica Morris and the reverend's children. The friction with the family, combined with the long hours and Frank's perfectionism, meant that tempers began to flare and conflicts arose in the workplace. Some of these were about money.

One dispute that Greta remembers was with Marcus over expenses. 'Bruce's expenses were paid, as were someone else's, some boy who had only just joined. I thought, Hold on. This isn't fair, and wrote to Marcus to claim my expenses. They got paid for a bit, until I got an explosive letter from Marcus saying they would be stopped and deducted from my wage.' Greta was always prepared to fight her corner, and this wasn't the only time they had words. Another disagreement was over a promised raise that never happened. 'A lot of things were promised and never happened.' She asked Accounts where the raise was, but they'd never heard of it. 'Marcus offered to lend me £10 but I didn't want a loan, I wanted the raise he had promised me, and eventually I got it.' Marcus offering the loan is quite typical and shows that he was not lacking in generosity, but wasn't always the most sensitive.

Marcus's duties were now such that it was impossible for him to carry on his work at St James's. He had tried to maintain his ministry even after the move south, but it was never going to be practical. He admitted defeat early in 1951 and gave his final sermon in April. At this point he was only editing *Eagle*, but just six months later the sister paper *Girl* was launched and Marcus was working as hard as anyone.

It was still the norm for everyone in the studio to be working sixteen-hour days, ending at two or three in the morning and returning a few hours later. When tiredness starts creeping in, fuses get shorter, and it was not long before mutterings began. In truth it would appear that it was nothing more than grumblings over the coffee pot, but to Frank it seemed more than that and he took it as a planned revolt against his leadership. When Eric Eden tried to discuss the long hours they were putting in, Frank took it as the team turning against him and decided that he could not allow it. He just couldn't understand why, if he was prepared to work until he dropped, his team would not. This was during 'The Red Moon Mystery', whose plot had bees using magnetic forces to steer the red moon in their search for food. With Ivor Dare's help Dan defeats them, but Frank would not let the bee of Eden's complaint out of his bonnet and insisted to Marcus that he be sacked. He could not, would not, be dissuaded. Eden got a job with an advertising agency, but that was not the last Dan Dare saw of him.

The workload continued to get tougher and tougher and with the pressure he put on himself it was almost inevitable that Frank would eventually crack. His first major illness came towards the end of 'The Red Moon Mystery'. No disrespect is intended to Harold Johns, but it is quite clear even to the casual observer that 'Marooned on Mercury', which followed straight on from 'Red Moon', does not have Frank Hampson at the artist's board. Frank had already had some time off due to illness during 'Voyage to Venus', but even though he is still credited as the artist on the Mercury story, his input was limited.

His ill-health during 'Venus' was put down to over-work and as 'Mercury' began it was credited to an inner-ear problem. One would normally expect this sort of thing to last a couple of days, but the fact that it rendered Frank useless for the whole of the Mercury story indicates deeper problems. No doubt these were related to fatigue and pressure, and he was again taken ill towards the end of the next story. The art for 'Mercury' was in the hands of Johns, with Tomlinson helping out. Frank didn't even write the scripts, a job that went to Chad Varah.

In his autobiography Varah tells us, 'My chief job on *Eagle* was as scientific and astronautical consultant to Dan Dare.' In effect the job he was given was to check that anything Frank came up with was possible within the realms of what was known about the universe at the time. It seems that he took this part of the role even further, making sure that Frank did not waste opportunities for later stories. He recounts one episode where Frank had Dan stopping on Mars on his way to Venus, and discovering that there was no life there although there had once been some. Varah pointed out that if the series was to run and run, they would one day need Mars and would most likely need some aliens on it.

Varah was a vital cog in the *Eagle* wheel, though his scriptwriting contribution to 'Dan Dare' itself was limited to 'Marooned on Mercury'. Because he had been working with Marcus for a number of years in the quest to push Christian publishing, he was very much Marcus's right-hand man and main sounding board. He also had the (un?)enviable task of trawling through all the unsolicited manuscripts sent in to the comic for possible publication. In fact, it was Varah who 'discovered' Arthur C. Clarke when he picked out the two stories sent by his agent. Varah wrote the double-page text story 'Plot Against the World' which appeared in Issue 1 and ran for seventeen weeks, and also scripted many of the early religious tales on the back page. He has described how onerous a task this was as he was only really working for the *Eagle* part-time. He hadn't got the time to plan the whole story – not unusual for anything connected with the *Eagle* – and never knew from one week to the next how his cliffhanger would continue. As well as his major contribution to the *Eagle* his lasting legacy is the Samaritans, which he founded in 1953.

With Varah scripting, Harold and Greta were the only two artists working on the 'Mercury' story, so it is no wonder that the quality slipped. It seems unfair to highlight this because at the height of the studio there had been up to seven people working on the art, and therefore it is almost inevitable that the work in this period suffered. One particular example is from early January 1953. It is not bad drawing as such, but the characters do not look like themselves. Also the level of detail that we had become used to has gone, as has the strict maintenance of light source and continuity. It is bad in comparison to what was expected, and highlights just how good the work was when it was done right.

The plot for 'Marooned on Mercury' was actually quite clever, in that it was a straight continuation from the previous tale, at the end of which, in saving the world, Dan, Digby, Peabody and Sondar had been blasted seemingly into oblivion. The penultimate frame of 'Red Moon' was a facsimile of a newspaper reporting their deaths.

On Mercury they discover their old enemy the Mekon up to his usual tricks, trying to regain his position of dominance by using slave Mercurian labour to produce the deadly panthanaton with which to hold the universe to ransom. In spite of the artwork not being up to Frank's standard, Harold created the memorable Mercurians. With the help of his new-found friends on Mercury, especially the incredibly strong Samson, Dan and the team are able to overcome the Mekon. It was hoped that Frank would be back soon; there was something missing when he was away, like the Factory without Andy Warhol, and so it was a relief to all that he returned full of vigour for 'Operation Saturn'. This turned into a fifteen-month extravaganza of a story and was the most ambitious so far, with the added element of the enemy coming from within.

It was at this time that Bruce Cornwell returned. He had left because of the 'murderously' heavy workload, so it was a surprise, to say the least, for him to come back and effectively replace Eric Eden, who had been sacked because of his own dissatisfaction with the number of hours they were working. He didn't just walk back in, though. It took a personal visit from Frank to persuade him, with promises that the workload was less (it wasn't), that the organisation would improve (it didn't) and that the deadlines weren't so tough (they were). Bruce quickly realised that returning was not a good decision, and left for a second time when he became ill due to the crazy workload on 'Operation Saturn'. The way he describes it, you can see why he had to leave.

It was really horrendous. I could leave here on a Monday [he lived in Ruislip and travelled to Epsom on his motorbike] and I wouldn't know when I'd be getting home again. That's how it was. I might make it in a working day or it might take two days before I got home again. In the end I said to him, 'Frank, I'm not well, I've seen the quack, he wants me to have a couple of weeks off. I haven't had any holidays yet, how about it?' So he said, 'Well, I'm not well either and if I can't have a holiday neither can you.' So that was it, I just walked out. Frank was under great strain, I knew that, but he couldn't handle people at all.

What he was asking, what he was trying to put on paper, was impossible for one person to do, he just couldn't manage. It's the type of artwork that required a hell of a lot of drawing, an awful lot of thought.

Bruce still feels it was a big mistake to come back:

I [shouldn't] have gone anywhere near it . . . Funnily enough, the characters from cartoons that I was raised with in the States, Frank knew about them all as well. We shared the same basic standards for cartooning, it wasn't a problem to me but associating with Frank was the first time I took to cartooning at all. Illustrating, yes, but not cartooning as such, and I had to wean myself off it after I left Frank. I didn't want to do it any more and I'm quite happy with the way I see things, but that first sort of [time] . . . [it was] a nightmare that's lived with me.

But then he finishes by saying, 'It was an experience and . . . it was good solid stuff and nothing to be ashamed of.' Asked what his best work on the strip was, he says with a laugh, 'All of it.'

It wasn't just the artists who were affected by the punishing workload. Frank's sister Margaret remembers travelling down from the north-west to visit her brother and his family in Epsom. It wasn't as easy a trip as it is now, and when she got there, 'I didn't see much of Frank because he was always working. There were so many deadlines, it was . . . it was horrific really. He worked himself to death, to be honest, to get the deadlines and to do it. So we didn't really see him, it was mostly Dorothy and Peter [who we saw], of course when he was a boy. We only saw Frank occasionally; he was always in his studio.'

Peter remembers that his father was practically always working.

My dad really didn't have a sort of work/social life, he just had a work life. He was at it all the time, he really was. We used to take a holiday every now and then, Christmas and stuff like that. If we weren't on holiday then the chances are he would be at work.

He did sketch a bit [on holiday]. We used to go to the Norfolk Broads; we went there a few times. He liked doing that sort of thing, on boats. He did some sketching while we were there and I've still got some of the pencil sketches he did while we were there. I think he was generally not unhappy to be away from a desk for a couple of weeks and not putting pencil to paper. But those sketches are great, they're really nice little pencil sketches of boats, buildings along the riverbank, that sort of thing.

. . . In one of his old sketchbooks, he must have sat in front of the television, because he was sketching the characters from the television. The panellists on *What's my Line?*, stuff like that. Gilbert Harding. So there are a few pictures there so I guess that must have been a time when he was watching telly and not working. They're old, probably 1952.

*

'Operation Saturn' introduced the world to the first 'Dan Dare' baddie that was not an alien. It was time to show the readers that evil lurks everywhere, even in your own back yard. And Blasco wasn't just human, he was a trusted scientist from within Space Fleet! Dr Blasco was important because it was his actions that drove the whole plot, from the invasion of the black cats, or 'kroopaks', as they were actually called on Saturn, right through to the dénouement, but he was interesting for another reason: he was the first villain to kill someone in cold blood. When a junior Space Fleet aide looks like he may have discovered something fishy in the luggage he's helping Blasco carry on to the ship, the evil doctor just runs his sword through him, from behind, without blinking an eye. No character had ever done this sort of thing before. Blasco engineers a trip to Saturn, with the aim of helping Vora with his quest for universal domination and in return being set up as the ruler of Earth. If not for Dan's intervention the whole world order would be upset.

The 'Saturn' story is Peter Hampson's favourite.

I'm not sure why, but I like certain aspects of that. I like Blasco, and the black cats. Later than that the Elektro-bots and the Selektrobots [in 'Reign of the Robots'].

Death was quite unusual. There were lots of fights and so on but not much actual death. Maybe that's why I liked Blasco. Also the Monatomic Hydrogen and all that. [Monatomic hydrogen was a highly unstable fuel, needed to power the ship that took the team the long distance to Saturn. A large section of the story is given over to the testing of this fuel.]

I love some of the artwork from that as well, because he experimented with scraper board and all sorts of stuff around that time and so some of that is really brilliant.

Since Frank generally based characters on real people, it is worth noting that Don Harley recalls seeing an early sketch of Dr Blasco with 'Cornwell' written next to it. So it would appear that Bruce Cornwell was also the enemy within . . .

But Cornwell wasn't the only one to jump ship. Two other artists left during Dan's trip to Saturn: Harold Johns and Greta Tomlinson. Frank showed a similar cold-bloodedness to Blasco: the most important thing in his life was Dan Dare, and nothing would get in the way of him making it the best strip in the world, even if it meant firing his oldest colleague, friend even.

Here's how Tomlinson remembers the end:

We got the sack, which came as a complete shock. By that time we were working mainly on the annual. And we suddenly found we weren't working at night and at the weekend and all night. And that felt very strange; we didn't know what to do with ourselves. So Harold said he was going to ring up Marcus, and 'ask him if it's OK if I apply for more work. And if you help, I'll pay you another £3 a week.' I was on £12 at this point, so this would have put me on £15. He started to do strips. I don't know who for. It might have been the *Lion*, I can't remember. And I helped with the figure work. We'd been doing it a few weeks when Harold got called for an interview with Marcus. I went to London with him and went shopping and bought the most expensive coat I'd ever bought, Aquascutum.

When they met up after the meeting, 'I could see from a mile off there was something wrong. So I said, "What's the matter?" He said, "I've got the sack." "What?" He said, "So have you." So I said, "What for?" He said, "For doing extra work." And I said, "I thought you'd cleared it." He said, "I did. But that's the excuse."'

One can't help being struck by the callousness and unfairness of this, but most of all the sheer craziness. Here were two excellent artists who had worked on the magazine since day one – before day one in Harold's case – being sacked for doing something for which they had permission. They had helped create the *Eagle*, worked ridiculous hours without complaint and shown incredible loyalty. Not only that, but Frank and Harold went way back; surely that meant something?

Tomlinson obviously thought so too, for a short time. 'I said, "Don't worry, Frank'll sort it out. He'll sort it out." But he didn't. So we began to realise that he wasn't bothered either if we went. He wasn't interested. So that, I thought, was a bit of a betrayal.' In spite of the manner of the end of their working relationship, Greta has fond memories of Frank: 'Frank was easy to get on with, [but] he was the boss, and he was ten years older. Having been through the war makes you grow up more quickly. And whatever he said went and that was it. You didn't question it. He had a good sense of humour. I don't think I ever had a cross word with him.'

Bruce Cornwell remembers the whole incident well: 'He didn't do Harold any favours. He sacked him and Greta. It was nothing to do with Marcus. Marcus was a smooth cookie, he looked after his own tail, and the management of the studio was purely Frank.'

Greta got a job as a fashion artist up in Yorkshire, but didn't settle because it was too cold. 'I was frozen stiff. It must have been in the winter.' She missed London and so found a job with an advertising agency that was doing work for ITV. She did the storyboards for commercials for products as varied as Lucozade, Colliers Suits and various cigarettes. This work was only short-lived, as she married a man who worked for BP, went out to Iraq with him and got a job as the local rep for Elizabeth Arden. She stills paints and draws today and has been exhibited in many galleries.

In the wake of these departures a depleted team

comprising Frank, Don and freelance Desmond Walduck produced 'Prisoners of Space'. Desmond Walduck had been used in the 1953 *Dan Dare Space Book* and helped out towards the end of 'Operation Saturn'. 'Prisoners of Space' coincided with another period of ill-health for Frank, and it is plain to see that most of it was drawn by Don and Desmond. Frank was still doing the scripting and providing preliminary artwork, but mainly from home.

Another significant event during this period was the move, in 1954, to Bayford Lodge, a purpose-built studio which also included living space for Frank and his family. Finally, over four years after it all began, the team had a workspace fit for the purpose. Joan Porter remembers the move as being quite remarkable. 'At last, everything under one roof for the first time. A great deal of work was accomplished here, a huge filing system created, and models made as needed.'

'Prisoners' saw the arrival of two more significant figures who would help shape the golden period of the strip, one a fictional character, the other a writer.

On the page we saw the introduction of Flamer Spry. Although Frank's son Peter was used as a reference for the character, according to Frank he was based on another boy. It was a deliberate decision to introduce some characters the same age as the average reader, and this story started at the Space Fleet Academy. Maybe, just maybe, thought the young readers, they would one day be able to go to a college to learn how to be Dan Dare. Putting the words into the mouth of young Flamer and his fellow recruits was Alan Stranks, who for the next six years would work with Frank on the scripts.

Stranks was already well known to *Eagle* readers as the writer of 'PC49', about a kindly copper on the beat, which he had transferred from radio to the pages of the comic. He also wrote the script for another *Eagle* strip, 'Mark Question', but it is his 'Dan Dare' work for which he will always be remembered. 'Prisoners' saw the return of the Mekon, and once his plot to kill Dan has been overcome he is captured. This really does seem to be the end of him. Digby suggests boiling him in oil, but Guest will not treat a prisoner of war like that. A Venusian jury decides his fate and he is sent to a rehabilitation centre. The Mekon knows he will not reform: 'End this farce, Earthmen! Torture and destroy me as I would have done you!' But they just won't listen to common Mekon sense.

While important for the introduction of Flamer, and notable for Stranks joining the team, 'Prisoners of Space' was actually rather run-of-the-mill. We had already seen the Mekon trying to use Dan to gain control of the world, and the constant stand-offs between the two had reached their natural conclusion. While it was inconceivable for the Mekon to be killed, which would have been against Dan's code and the justice system of the world, it was definitely time for him to be put out of the way so that Dan could branch out. 'Prisoners' is not a bad story, but it feels slightly as if it is going through the motions, as if the creative team are ready for something big and they just need to get this story out of the way before they can embark on it.

That 'something big' was the trilogy that began with

'The Man from Nowhere'. By this stage things had settled down in the team. With Stranks and Frank looking after the plot and script, backed up by an excellent, and by now very experienced, artistic team of Don Harley, Eric Eden and Joan Porter, the stage was set for what was to become the strip's seminal trio of adventures. This team had five years' experience of producing a weekly strip so the process was routine, though still tough, and everyone knew what they were doing and what was expected of them. With Stranks to share the scriptwriting duties, Frank had time for plot development and planning each week's pages properly.

A recently discovered document which details Frank's early thoughts on 'Saturn' shows how much work had to be done, from the initial idea to getting the story on the printed page. It also highlights how much of the plot is changed during the process. By the time of 'The Man from Nowhere', this is being done by Frank and Stranks and, two heads being better than one, led to a more streamlined journey and better results.

This stability is reflected in the flow of the output that begins with 'The Man from Nowhere' and segues into 'Rogue Planet', then 'The Reign of the Robots' and the short 'Ship that Lived'. This continuing adventure ran from 13 May 1955 until 18 April 1958. For almost three years the same team kept the ball in the air, with a plot that thrilled and artwork of such quality that, if you are lucky enough to find it at auction, will fetch up to £7,500 for a single page.

These adventures took the core team of Dan, Digby, O'Malley and Flamer to the far-off planet of Cryptos at the behest of Lero, an envoy sent across the universe to bring Dan to save his people. The MacGuffin that keeps this story flowing into the following chapters is that while Lero has told them that his ship can travel at almost the speed of light and thus reach his home planet in a relatively short time, he has in fact put them in suspended animation for the five years it really takes. He only tells them this after they have helped him overcome the murderous Phants and are about to head back to Earth.

The conflict between the Phants and the Crypts is fuelled by their conflicting diets – food is still an important theme. The Phants consume a drug that makes them aggressive, while the Crypts are supplementing their food with a pill that makes them passive. The solution is a relatively easy one for Dan, much easier in fact than delivering the news to his men, and boy, that they have already been away from Earth for five years, which will become ten by the time they get home.

Both the script and the artwork for 'Man from Nowhere' and 'Rogue Planet' show the team at their peak. The villains are beautifully drawn and instantly frightening, from the towering Gogol through to the Kruels, the warrior priests of Orak. Given that the Kruels are only seen in three episodes of 'Rogue Planet' it is a mark of the quality of their creation that they are so memorable. It almost seems a waste to have them in for so short a time.

Every frame throughout these three tales is packed full, with characters drawn to perfection, and vast landscapes with so much background detail that you could spend hours looking at each scene. An excellent example comes from one page of 'Rogue Planet' dated 27 January 1956. There are only two frames. The first has a close-up of Dan and O'Malley as they survey the enemy position. The trials they have already been through show in their faces, as do the difficulties they are about to undergo. The second frame shows us what they can see. The Phants are loading their ships, readying their armies, preparing for war. You can feel the buzz of activity coming off the page.

The writing is excellent too, and reflects the anxieties of the times. The brain behind the Phants and the Kruels is Orak. Dan discovers that Orak is merely a super-computer, running on transistors which never wear out, and thus the 10,000-year cycle of hate and destruction between the Phants and the Crypts could go on for ever. In the real world of the 1950s, while it was true that the war had been won thanks to the help of computers, there was already a fear that automation was going to take over people's lives and leave us all at the mercy of machines. It is a theme often used in science fiction, the most popular being the *Terminator* series of films, in which a defence system created to protect Earth from attack turns on the very humans who created it.

The third part of the trilogy is 'Reign of the Robots'. The crew have been away for ten years and obviously expect much to have changed on Earth, but they could never have guessed what has actually happened. They land at a deserted Space Fleet HQ and head down to London, where they discover the Mekon in the holiest and most secret place, 'the Sanctum'. In a script that

A Phant slave transport. The detail even goes so far as working out how storage boxes would be piled (see over page).

The cover of one of the studio's roughs and ideas books. This book covers the period of the 'Rogue Planet' adventure.

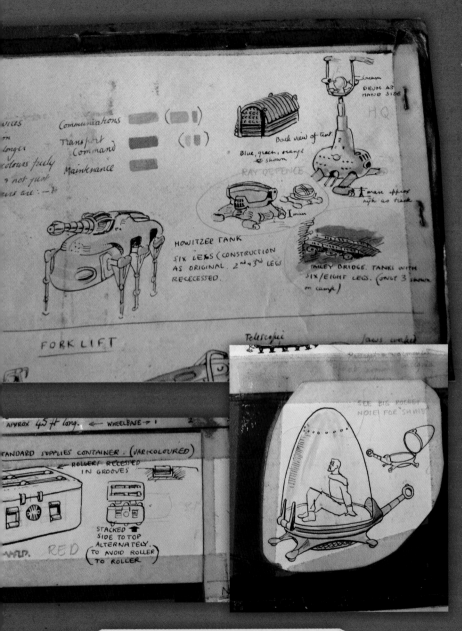

Communications

Transport
Command

Maintenance

Back view of tent.

Blue, green, orange
as shown

DRUM AS
HAND SIDE

HQ

RAY DEFENCE

HOWITZER TANK

SIX LEGS (CONSTRUCTION
AS ORIGINAL. 2nd & 3rd LEGS
RECECESSED.

1 man

1 man approx
high as track

BAILEY BRIDGE. TANKS WITH
SIX/EIGHT LEGS. (ONLY 3 shown
in camp)

FORK LIFT

Telescopic

Jaws curled

APPROX 45 ft long. ← WHEELBASE → 1

STANDARD SUPPLIES CONTAINER. (VARICOLOURED)

ROLLERS RECESSED
IN GROOVES

STACKED
SIDE TO TOP
ALTERNATELY.
TO AVOID ROLLER
TO ROLLER

RED

SEE BIG POCKET
NOTE) FOR 'SHINE'

Dan in his glass cage, and more
amazing technology and weaponry.

Engineers.

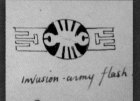

Invasion · army flash.

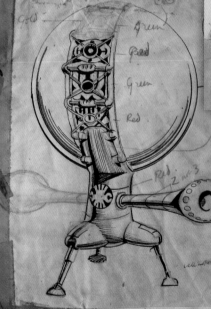

Tank Corps.

Space crew
Transport Command.

Detailed insignia and small elements of decorative design add to the depth of the world created.

Gogol's ship and loading platform.

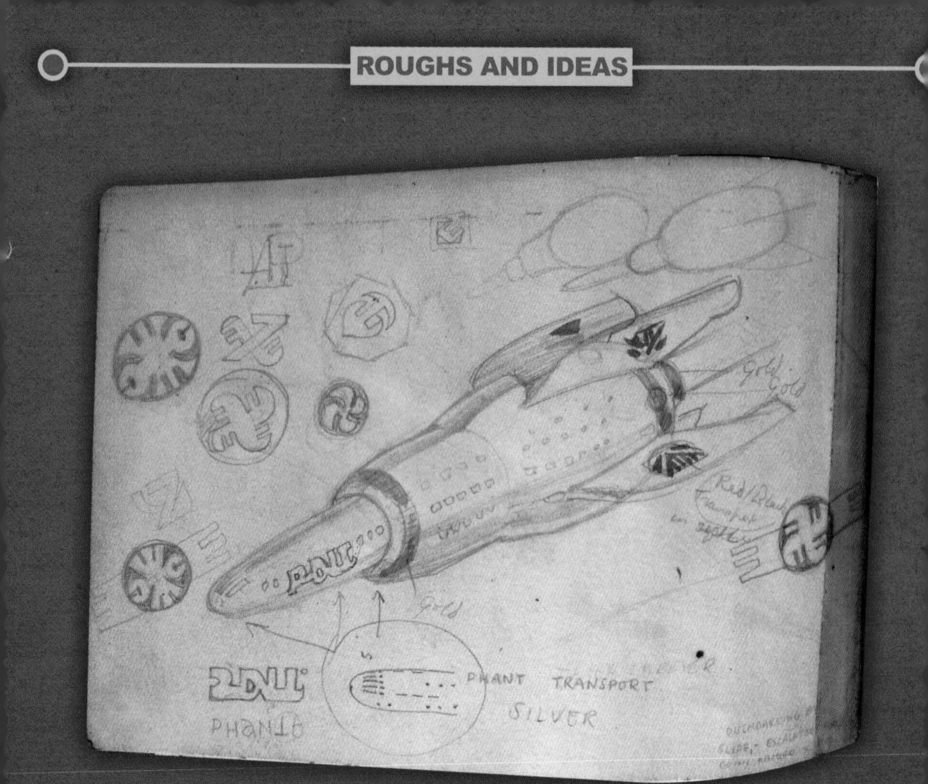
Gold
Gold
PHANT TRANSPORT
SILVER
PHANTO

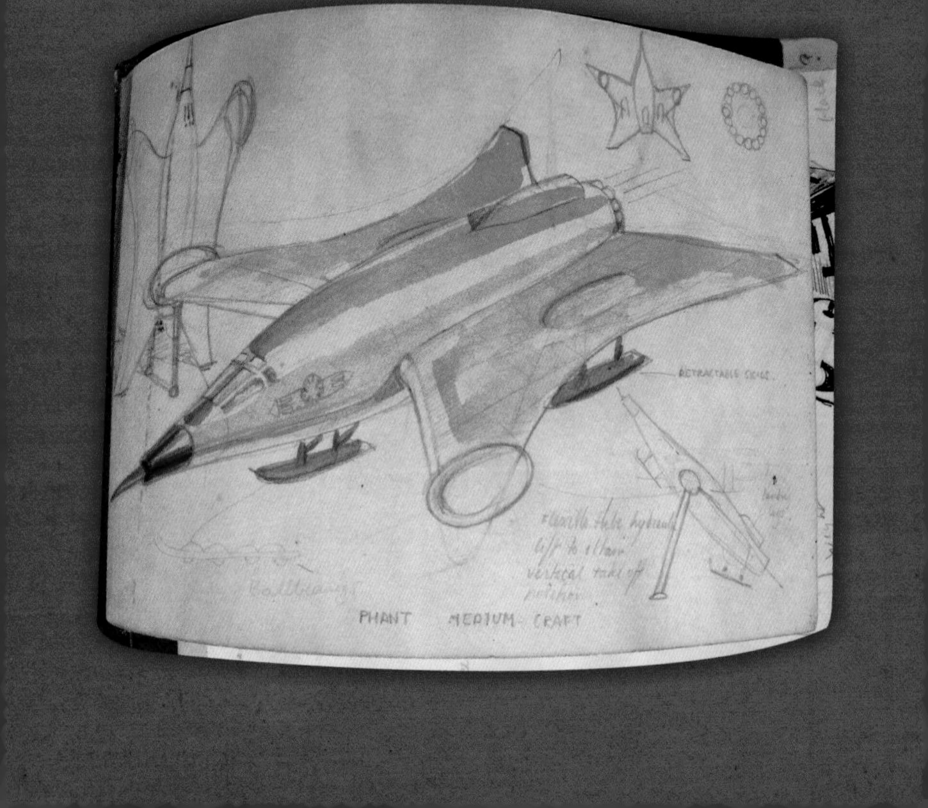
RETRACTABLE SKIDS
PHANT MEDIUM CRAFT

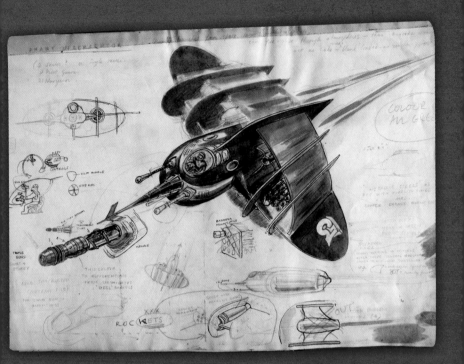

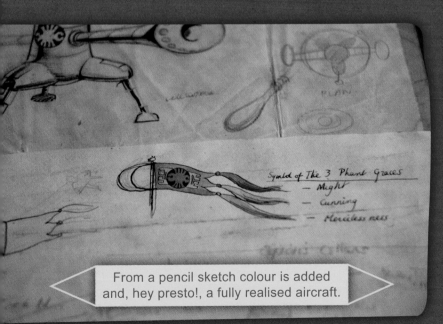

From a pencil sketch colour is added and, hey presto!, a fully realised aircraft.

Notes from Frank Hampson to Desmond Walduck.
Note that this drawing was done 'in a hurry' and
still looks like a work of art.

is in many ways the culmination of everything that has happened since the first story, he has been waiting for ten years for Dan's return and has used the time to take over Earth and use its inhabitants in a number of cruel experiments to recreate man's greatest achievements. His aims as ever are purely scientific: he just wants to establish and record how all the major discoveries of mankind were made. In battling and overcoming the green meanie and his élite force of practically indestructible Selektrobots, Dan hopes that once again peace can be returned to the world. This of course could never happen, either in the *Eagle* or at Hulton Press.

'The Ship that Lived' was a short add-on at the end of 'Reign of the Robots', mainly about saving the seemingly doomed *Anastasia* and showing the Mekon apparently disappearing to an unknown death. It is followed by 'The Phantom Fleet', a tale that begins excellently, with some fascinating new spaceships appearing out of nowhere, but ends with a whimper. Marcus Morris rarely interfered with 'Dan Dare', but in this case he felt the story was a little dull and wanted it cut short. Reading it now, one can't help feeling he was wrong. The Cosmobes, who have come to Earth seeking help and refuge, are a nice creation, as is their predicament. They are a water-dwelling race, but the water has run out. With today's problems of global warming, melting ice-caps, unpredictable and destructive weather patterns and natural disasters, there could have been a lot to learn. Frank probably acceded to Morris's demand because he had lined up his next 'great' plot and was eager to get started. But unfortunately for him, the calm of the previous five years was about to be broken and he and the team would be rocked by events that would change their world, Dan's world and the *Eagle* for ever.

'Safari in Space' was meant to be the start of the next great series of adventures as Dan went looking for his dad, William, across the universe. Frank had it all mapped out, as far as these things were ever fully mapped out, and the future looked bright. In March 1959's *Eagle* Dan Dare and the crew are right in the middle of their safari in space and in trouble as always. They have been kidnapped by the eccentric scientist Galileo McHoo. He tells them that Dan's father might not be dead, and that he, McHoo, needs their help to find out what has happened to William Dare and his own uncle, Copernicus McHoo, and the revolutionary ship, the *Galactic Pioneer*, built by McHoo's father. But back in the offices of the *Eagle*, Frank and his crew were about to be kidnapped by an eccentric publisher in search of bigger profits and world domination.

The purchaser was Odhams Press, which, worried about the recent acquisition of Amalgamated Press by the *Daily Mirror*, decided it needed some instant growth to fight off any potential buyers. As well as *Eagle*, Hulton's main assets were *Lilliput* (one of the original inspirations for *The Anvil*) and *Picture Post*. The former was a showcase for short stories, comic writing and coverage of the arts, while the latter was at the forefront of photojournalism. By the end of the 1950s *Picture Post* had ceased publication, and Marcus Morris had been given the job of trying to revive a shabby-looking *Lilliput*.

With two of its three big names in trouble, Hulton had not paid dividends to its shareholders the previous year, and so the £1.8 million offer was hard to resist.

On the face of it, this shouldn't have been a major problem for the 'Dan Dare' team. Here they were, producing the main strip in the flagship publication for the company; surely they would be left alone to carry on the good work? After all, everything was quite settled, they had a method and a product to be proud of. They could not have been more wrong.

Timing is everything; not long before the Odhams takeover, Frank had been promised some time off by Marcus. He was to use it for rest and recuperation, and also for a research trip to America to look at both comics and rockets, still his passion. This sabbatical had not been rubber-stamped by the big-wigs by the time of the change of ownership, and the promise made by Marcus under the old regime had to be sold to the new one. They refused point-blank. The main reason Marcus had given in to Frank's demand was that rivals Amalgamated had offered him a job at a much better salary. Marcus knew how important Frank was to 'Dan Dare' – at one time Frank was insured for £150,000 – and so was ready to do what he could to keep him on board. Another part of the deal to keep Frank at the *Eagle* was that he would not have to do any more drawing on 'Dan Dare'. Frank wanted to be in control of the strip and felt that to do so properly he needed more time to plan stories, create characters and oversee the others' work. The time he spent working at his board was not allowing him to do this.

The decision by the Odhams hierarchy to refuse

Frank's trip caused embarrassment to Marcus, and a consequent loss of face and power. This was the beginning of death by a thousand cuts for Marcus's relationship with his new bosses. The next was the imposition of a fixed-figure expense account, which went against his existing agreement but was in line with Odhams' practices. It soon became apparent that they would not be able to work together, and in September 1959, just six months after the takeover, Marcus was gone. His final letter from the editor's office appeared in the *Eagle* on 31 October 1959. His name stayed on the comic for quite a while as he was credited as the writer of 'The Road of Courage'. (Even though it now appears he didn't write it. That job was actually undertaken by the Reverend Guy David as Marcus had already started working elsewhere. Revd David was never credited because Odhams insisted upon keeping Marcus's byline in the comic, at least for a while after he had left.)

The pressure on Frank during this time is easy to understand. Since the *Eagle* had begun, he had been the main man. It was he and Marcus who created the magazine and he who still ran the most important strip. For ten years Marcus had left him to his own devices and hardly ever interfered with the strip, other than an occasional nudge here or there, but when Marcus left Frank was exposed to the decision-making of people he believed had no idea what they were dealing with in trying to publish a boys' comic. His control was taken away, his methods were under question, and promises made to him by the previous management had been reneged upon.

Greta Tomlinson remembers seeing him some time after he left the *Eagle*, when the after-effects of the whole experience were obviously still very much in evidence. In her opinion he seemed to have had a complete break-down. She couldn't believe it.

> I went to visit him, after I'd been abroad. How insecure he was; he was a completely different person. He'd completely lost confidence. He said, 'I'll never draw again, Greta.' It took my breath away. I said, 'You're brilliant, what do you mean? You're absolutely fantastic, of course you will.' 'Don't think so, don't think so.' Whether that was when he found he'd lost the copyright, and I believe they treated him disgracefully, I think it was something to do with that. It destroyed him, it really did.

Things came to a head when Frank discovered that Odhams, having only owned the rights for the blink of an eye, were in discussions about producing a film of Dan Dare's adventures. He could not believe that he hadn't been consulted and was to have no involvement. If he had known that, even fifty years later, a film would still not have been made, he may have felt glad to have been left out of the loop, but as it was he was left feeling totally deflated and undervalued. So he made the decision to step away from his baby altogether.

While his promised trip to the States was important to him, and more than anything else he needed the break, it appears that the main reason for his departure was a feeling that 'Dan Dare' was no longer his. He had begun to feel bitter about being treated as just a paid flunkey, not given the respect he deserved as the creator. It wasn't just that he no longer had 'Dan Dare'; he had big plans way beyond the *Eagle*, plans that he had harboured since day one on *The Anvil*.

'I needed a break, certainly from Dare. The plan was that I should do something else for a year and then return to Dare. But the basic trouble was that there was, for me, always a canker in the apple with Dan Dare.' Frank saw from the very start that there would be great commercial exploitation possible from the strip, and this would enable him to build a large studio of artists, which would lead to further activities, along similar lines to the American animation studios, giving him a chance to break the US comic and animated-film market. 'It was a logical progression ... to building something really big. Unfortunately for me the circumstances of *Eagle*'s production made it impossible for me to retain the copyright and therefore control.'

He had already tried to implement his ideas, with no success, and as soon as Hulton hit financial trouble it was pretty much the end for him.

I went off Dare in 1959 in order to do a life of Christ, which I'd always thought we ought to do because at least that was the reason the thing had started. And when I came back it was to a completely different set-up, different firm, different people, and although I completed that strip ['The Road of Courage'], after it I felt there was no . . . they suggested I should do a strip called . . . I forget what it was called, but it was about a Victorian trumpeter who was illegitimate and it just didn't fit with *Eagle* at all. It was rubbish. It was the kind of thing that AP [Amalgamated Press] had been doing for years and years and years under Leonard Matthews. It was a very, very unhappy time for me. Towards the end I was treated like an office boy . . . I tried to commit suicide . . . but Dorothy came home, she'd forgotten her gloves.

It was almost a year before the final appearance of 'Hulton Press Ltd' at the foot of the front page, but the changes had already begun to bite hard and deep. Behind the scenes very little was left of the studio team that Frank had spent ten years creating. Frank himself was gone, Joan Porter was gone, Eric Eden was gone and scriptwriter Alan Stranks was gone (he died June 1959). A team that had worked together for five years was dismantled in a few months, and while Don Harley was still there, the strip was never the same again.

CHAPTER FIVE

Frank Bellamy's
Non-Studio System

CLIFFORD MAKINS took over from Marcus but found the 'Dan Dare' department much depleted.

With Frank's departure, Frank Bellamy was brought in as lead artist. He began his association with the *Eagle* indirectly, by working for its sister paper *Swift*. From there he moved to the *Eagle*, where he rose to prominence with his colour strip about the life of Churchill, 'The Happy Warrior'. His individual style was really shown here and he went on to tell the life story of King David. Not long after starting on 'Marco Polo' he got the call to take over from Frank Hampson, partway through 'Terra Nova'. The two Franks never worked on the strip at the same time, but it was Hampson who recommended Bellamy as his successor. He had obviously seen Bellamy's work on the aforementioned strips and was sufficiently impressed to think he would do a good job with 'Dare'.

They may have shared a first name but their styles of drawing could not have been more different, and this does raise the question of why Hampson recommended him. The only logical answer is that Hampson believed that Bellamy would not be a threat to his own position of head artist on the comic. When he first stepped down from 'Dare' it was with the intention of returning after a year or so away, and Bellamy only signed on for a year. Had Hampson recommended Don Harley, he may have worried the bosses would see that someone cheaper and quicker could produce what he did.

Frank Hampson has often been quoted as saying that Don Harley was the second best 'Dan Dare' artist (after himself, of course). The reason Don didn't get the job was probably because his style was too similar to Frank's. Odhams felt Frank's style was outdated and dull, and so it was to Frank Bellamy that they turned.

With instructions from above to make 'Dare' his own, Bellamy wasted no time in stamping his own imprint on the strip, even though he took over halfway through a story. There was a printers' strike in the middle of 1959, meaning Hampson's last two covers are undated, but they are Volume 10, nos. 26 and 27, and show him still on top form. No. 28, dated 29 August 1959, has the first Bellamy cover and the change in style is obvious. He didn't sign it, though, because it is clear that in his early covers he was actually trying to continue the Hampson style a little. The first pages he puts his signature to are dated 3 October. Up till this point he had been doing one page and Don Harley had been doing the other, but for no. 33 he did both, and signed them, and it is clear that he was now stamping his imprint on the strip.

Bellamy's style was all action and movement, and it

is noticeable from the moment he takes over not just that Dan looks different but that the whole dynamic of the strip changes. Those two pages on 3 October 1959 are classic examples of this difference, not just in the drawing but in the draughtsmanship. The second page has a splintered circular panel showing O'Malley being caught by the giant Nagrab ants; it is tinted by the red and orange glow of O'Malley's blazing gun.

Here we come to a bone of contention among 'Dan Dare' fans. Those who have been fans of the strip since day one are in no doubt that Hampson produced the greatest strips of their kind, and certainly the definitive Dan. The shame is that Frank Bellamy was a brilliant artist who brought his characters as much to life as his predecessor ever did, just in a different way. His Dan seems older, wiser and more hardened. Every slight, punch, trauma, is etched into his features. It is not a case of one Frank being better than the other; they were just totally different. Comparing Bellamy's Dan to Hampson's is pointless, like comparing an apple to a shoe.

It was not just the style of his drawing that differed. Bellamy did not believe in the studio system: he felt that a single artist should draw the whole strip from his head, 'mind-drawing', as Hampson would have called it. The photographs, the models, the dressing up were in his opinion a waste of time, effort and money. In this he had no arguments from the bosses at Odhams. If Bellamy could produce a strip for less money they were going to take it. There is a story that Don Harley ordered the very first page he produced to be reworked, but eventually he was pretty much left in total control and, with Don assisting, produced 'Terra Nova', 'Trip to Trouble' and 'Project Nimbus', all scripted by Eric Eden.

One thing that is very noticeable in Bellamy's time at the helm is the difference between his work and that of his assistants. From one page to the next it looks like a totally different strip. While during Hampson's time there were occasions when the difference between one of his frames and one from his assistants was noticeable, it was never so striking. The discrepancies appearing now can't have helped lock in readers. With the continuity he sometimes achieved by doing both pages in the same issue, Bellamy's work is stunning. No, it's not Hampson's Dare, but it would be harsh on Bellamy to say this period was the termination of the character.

According to Don Harley, 'Frank [Bellamy] worked at his home in Morden, not with us in the studio. He came to visit once or twice a week, and told us what he wanted us to do.' The team of Eric, Frank and Don were still producing two full colour pages a week to the same deadlines as under Hampson, but the way Don remembers it, life seemed less stressful. It is obvious the affection Don has for Bellamy and the times they shared: 'He was a small man, smaller than me and I'm quite short, and very funny. A bit like Norman Wisdom. He just made us laugh all the time. He was always the main attraction in any room he entered.'

In contrast, Bruce Cornwell recalled of Frank Hampson, 'I remember when the studio moved near Shoe Lane. There was a canteen on the top floor of this building. It was all sort of fixed tables and chequered covers on top.

Frank said, "I can't eat with you lot." I was horrified. I thought, My God, man, what are you on about? So he separated himself. There was three or four of us in the team, we all ate happily together and Frank was off somewhere else.' Frank Hampson was not a bad person, but he clearly felt he needed to maintain his status within his team.

There were two main differences that now allowed the strip to be produced much faster. First, there were no more constant rewrites and changes in what was required. Once the script was written, and Bellamy had decided what needed drawing, they stuck to it. Second, they didn't spend time on the photographic-reference stage that was so central to the way Hampson worked. He would never have accepted some of the frames that Bellamy turned in. For example, on the 3 October cover there is a panel with Professor Peabody and Flamer Spry looking on as O'Malley battles the giant Nagrab ants on Terra Nova. These creatures are scary in any light, and Bellamy really brings them to life, but there is something not quite right. Spry, on the right of the frame, is in front of Peabody and the light is hitting the left side of his face. In isolation he looks fine, and the shadows on his face are correct. But Peabody, just behind him and to his right, should be totally in shadow, yet somehow her face is lit as though the light source has gone through Spry's head. Also the reflection of light in her eyes is wrong. It looks like there are two light sources, one to the left and one to the right of her, but the right side of her face is in shade. This, Hampson would have said, is the problem when you don't use proper reference photographs. This, Bellamy and Odhams would have said, is irrelevant because here is a frame drawn in a fraction of the time and at a fraction of the cost, which is both dynamic and arresting.

While Bellamy's new style is obvious from that very first page he worked on, he made an even bigger change when it came to working on his first full adventure. Although 'Trip to Trouble' is a story in its own right, it forms the third part of a trilogy with 'Safari in Space' and 'Terra Nova', and so it was not until 'Project Nimbus' that Bellamy totally rewrote the 'Dan Dare' style book. As he had signed on for just a year, this was also his last 'Dan Dare' adventure, but he really went to town.

This wasn't just Bellamy's doing though, as a major revamp was under way, to be launched on 19 March 1960. In the run-up to the revamp, the readers were given the chance to have their say. Under a headline of WE WANT TO KNOW!, readers were encouraged to return a coupon indicating the two features they liked the least and to suggest replacements. This was rather pompously referred to as 'the *Eagle* Contents Election'. The 'election' coincided with the announcement of the decision to close the Eagle Club. The reason given was that the 'main activities have, for some time now, been extended to all readers', by which it was meant that everything was available to all readers without the need for membership. The club had always been something special, something that a member could use to put himself above the casual reader. With its passing the comic lost that important link with its most ardent followers. The Eagle Club had made them feel good about themselves. It was like that moment at a concert when the singer catches your eye, even for a tiny moment: it makes you feel as though the concert is just for you. Whether this was another money-saving move, or an indication that club membership had dropped off anyway, it was a fundamental change in the nature of the comic.

It is worth taking a moment to see what changed in the magazine as a whole by comparing the contents for 12 and 19 March 1960. There were three brand-new strips: 'Knights of the Road' told tales of life in a haulage company; 'Vic Venture' was a young lad who got into scrapes and on the back page was the much-heralded return of Frank Hampson with 'The Road of Courage', which would tell the story of the life of Jesus. By reading through the collected magazines in a bound volume you get to see Hampson's work directly opposite that of Bellamy. The comparison serves them both well, as you see instantly Hampson's eye for detail, character and plot whilst on the opposite page Bellamy's Dare shows vigour and movement.

Now that Bellamy was allowed to start from scratch, out went the Second World War-style Space Fleet uniforms, and in came what can best be described as a New Romantic style, the sort of thing the early Spandau Ballet probably based their wardrobe on. The Hampson reference books had built up all the ranks and insignia, much like a real army or air force, but Bellamy started again, and even introduced his own version of the Space Fleet badge, very similar to the uniform badges in *Star Trek*. He seems to be trying to find a different future, probably because his idea of the future is based on an early-1960s viewpoint, whereas Hampson's was rooted on the late 1940s. The designs are more futuristic, the spaceships look more like Concorde than space versions of Second World War craft.

An even more startling move was the ditching of Peabody, O'Malley and Flamer Spry, almost as though they hadn't spent the last few years trying to save the world. Peabody and Flamer play their full parts in 'Terra Nova' and then, without a by your leave, they are not in 'Trip to Trouble' and we never see them again. (Actually we do see Peabody one more time. In 'The Mushroom' a holidaying Hank Hogan meets up with Dan in London. They reminisce about old times and Hogan informs Dan that Jocelyn is now Mrs Jack Gurk. Dan looks silently into the distance, as though a small piece of his heart has been broken off. If he was that bothered, how come he didn't notice that she and Flamer had been left on Terra Nova when he, Digby and O'Malley went gallivanting off to find his father?)

O'Malley didn't look back either, but he needn't have felt so smug. Once Dan had discovered his father was dead in 'Trip to Trouble', it was *adios* to O'Malley without so much as a wave or a 'See you later'. He did turn up again in 'The Earth Stealers' and then 'Give Me the Moon', but he was ousted from the inner circle. These departures made the strip into more of a double act between Dare and Digby rather than the ensemble piece it had been before.

The front page was totally redesigned and the world said goodbye to the familiar large red panel, which became a banner right across the top. There is one large panel

AND SO THE RANGER, CARRYING DAN'S SMALL ROCKET SHIPS LEAVES THE EARTH ON THE FIRST STAGE OF THE DANGEROUS TRIP TO VENUS

WE'VE MADE IT, SIR! WE'RE AWAY!

...ysterious objects ...own as Black Cats ...e appeared on Earth – ...d by rulers of an Empire ...habiting the nine moons of ...urn. The spaceship *Val-*...e, under command of Dan ...re, flies to Saturn to inves-...ate. Chief scientist aboard, ...Blasco, is secretly in league ...h the Saturnians. Helped by ...ck Cats (electronic brain police ...chines), he seizes control of the ...p, but Dan and Digby escape in a ...all two-seater spaceship and make ...r Phoebe, Saturn's outermost moon.

CUT ROCKETS!

CHANGE OVER TO HOMING POWER!

THE STORY SO FAR: Colonel Dan Dare, Commander Lex O'Malley, young "Flamer" Spry and Spaceman Digby take off from Experimental Station X1 in the rebuilt Crypt ship with Lero, bound for the mystery planet Cryptos, five light years distant. To combat the fearful acceleration of the faster-than-light craft, Dan and his friends are clad in Crypt space-suits and embedded in counter-acceleration "coffins". As the ship approaches "Licht One" – the speed of light – anxious eyes watch from Earth, and the four volunteers, in their separate "cells", ponder the same fantastic problem . . .

The Ranger is the first ship we see Dan fly in, but he is not the pilot.

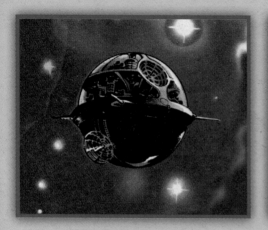

SUFFERING SATELLITES, SIR — *WHAT'S THAT?*

Frank Hampson didn't invent satellites but he took them further than anyone else.

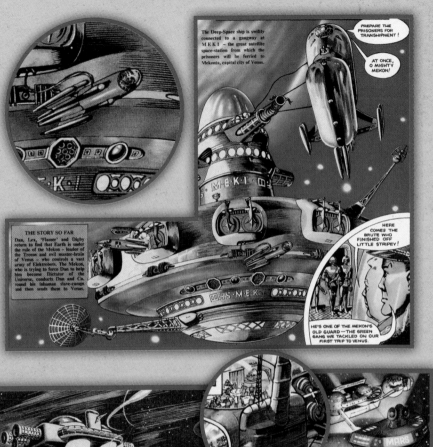

Did Frank Hampson invent the space station?

Weird and wonderful craft from the
Bayford Lodge Ideas book.

Dan and Digby fly by helicab in an effort to catch the *Valiant* before she sails for Saturn. Approaching Black Cat Island, they hear over the cab's radio the steady rhythm of the Take-Off Count, and see ahead of them the massive tower of the reinforced Landing Ramp.

KEY TO NUMBERS ON LAUNCHING RAMP
(1) Barrel. (2) Anti-flash vane and ring. (3) Booster ports. (4) Recoil cavity. (5) Recoil jack. (6) Shell. (7) Pressure tank. (8) 'Valiant'. (9) Control tower. (10) Double skin. (11) Lifting arms (hydraulic). (12) Air and gravity lock (disengaged position). (13) Recoil jack. (14) Rocket carriage in stowed position. (15) Cooling and anti-flash flanges. (16) Lift. (17) Primary booster. (18) Auto-pumproom. (19) Inner wall. (20) Outer wall.

The cutaway was a mainstay of *Eagle* so readers were used to its intricacies.

A vision in the water, soon to be a danger in the skies.

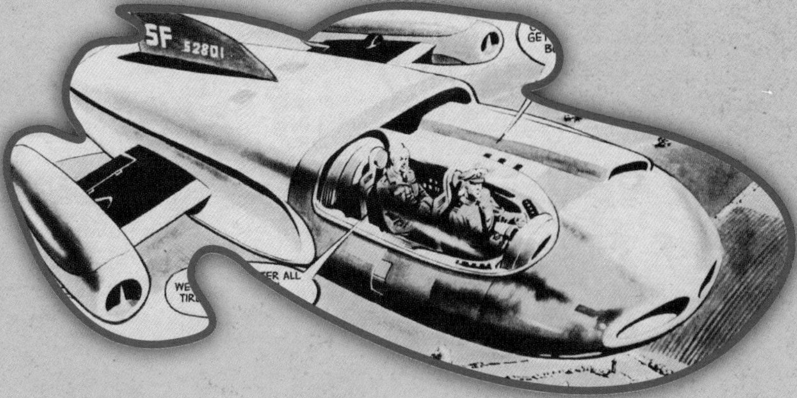
SF 52801

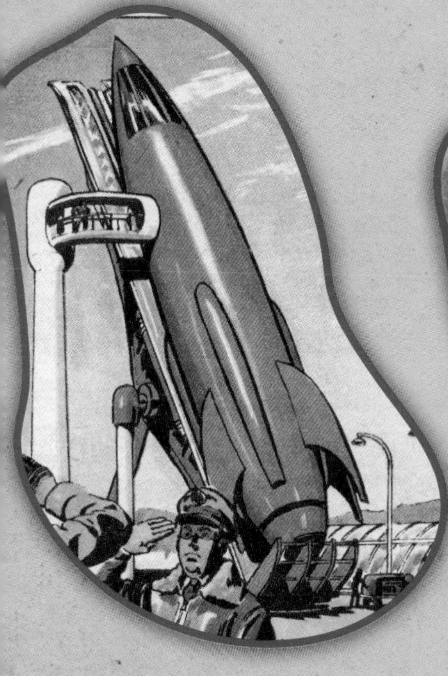

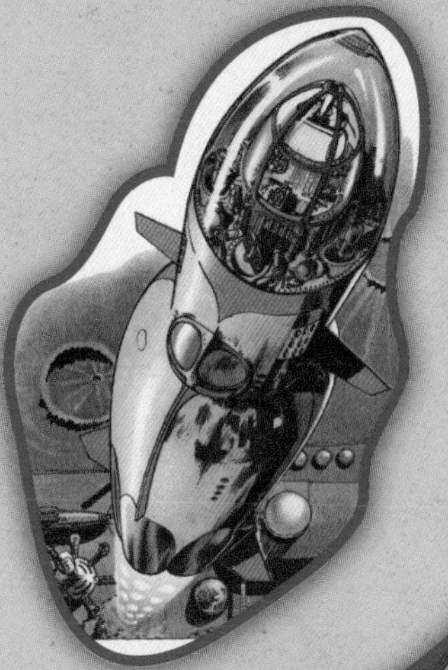

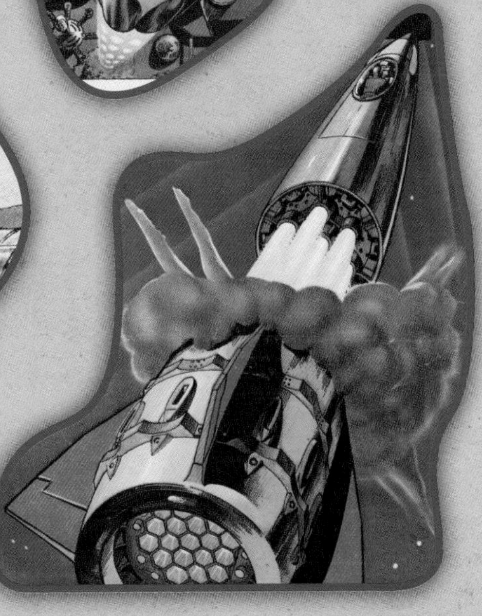

Light years ahead of any other
spaceship designer in the universe.

dominating the page, and four smaller ones which get the story moving. The story only runs for sixteen weeks and is not particularly memorable. A prototype ship, the *Nimbus One*, disappears. Dan and Digby go in search of it, come across some rather poor, easily defeated aliens who eat too much food too quickly and get tummy ache, find the *Nimbus* and bring it back.

And before you know it the Bellamy revolution is over with the end of his one-year contract. He went on to produce much stunning work for the *Eagle* in both his factual, historical strip about 'Montgomery of Alamein' and his award-winning fictional strips 'Fraser of Africa' and 'Heros the Spartan'. The work in these three strips offers a blueprint for many of today's graphic novels, both in the visceral strength of the imagery and in the imaginative use of framing. When he finally left the *Eagle* he did a stint with *TV21*, by now a well-trodden path for ex-Eaglers, before garnering further acclaim on 'Garth' for the *Daily Mirror*.

Since Bellamy had been brought in to revamp 'Dan Dare' and make it more exciting, it is odd that there was no real attempt to carry on in this vein once he was gone. His departure left a vacuum which was filled by Don Harley, who had not previously been seen as up to the task of taking over, and Bruce Cornwell, returning seven years after he'd last left. These two artists were both great craftsmen in their own right, but their best work on 'Dan Dare' had been as assistants, taking their lead from the head artist.

Their reign began in July 1960 with 'Mission of the

Earthmen' and ran until 'The Earth Stealers' in March 1962. Eric continued in the scriptwriting chair. All four tales from this period have promising plots, but all of them fizzle out, with the resolution being a little too easy and convenient.

'Mission of the Earthmen' has Dan and Digby trying to bring peace to two warring tribes on a far-off planet. They succeed by in effect telling both sides that they will only leave them alone if they stop fighting. 'The Solid Space Mystery' begins with a great premise and also sees the long-awaited return of the Mekon: surely this heralds a return to form? Unfortunately not. The Mekon has created a field of solid space through which it was impossible to fly. Flights of vital supplies on the old Venus route are disrupted and the future of the Earth is again in question. The solution is discovered frustratingly easily, when Dan's new spaceship, a gift from the grateful folk he helped in the previous adventure, holds the key to flying through solid space. This disappointment is down to Eric Eden's scripts, and continues in 'The Platinum Planet', which has the boys entering a world where the inhabitants are ruled by 'mind waves'; they destroy the transmitter and everyone is free.

Eric's final attempt was 'The Earth Stealers', where Dan and Digby find, on their return from the Platinum Planet, that Earth is deserted. Echoes here for the readers of when the boys had returned to Earth after 'Rogue Planet', only to be plunged into the nightmare that was the 'Reign of the Robots'. Surely this was Eric's chance to plug into the history of Space Fleet and bring back the glory years. Sadly, another opportunity was missed, like a brilliant footballer who beats everybody with lovely footwork and dribbling, only to lose his nerve when he sees the goal. In this instance Earth has been evacuated due to a plague, and the person managing the clear-up has invented a drug with which he can control people's minds. Dan switches this drug with water and thus defeats him. The artwork throughout the period is fine but it no longer has the real excitement that 'Dan Dare' had come to stand for. It seems that, as Don once said, it was just a job.

Perhaps the quality of scripts was down to the fact that Eric Eden was a novice in the job. He'd only previously ever done the artwork and, as Greta and Harold found when they were given 'Rob Conway' in the early days of the *Eagle*, it is not so easy to do. His set-ups were good and imaginative, but he didn't have the writing skills to sustain them and see them through. This lull lasted throughout Eric's time until he went back to the drawing board at – where else? – *TV21*.

It was also during this period, on 21 October 1961 to be precise, that Dan lost his coveted spot as occupier of the full front cover. On that date *Eagle* introduced, on the left half of the cover, 'Men of Action'. It was a large single-panel drawing with some text underneath, and the debutant was Stirling Moss. So maybe Don, Bruce and Eric were simply reacting to the way they, and their strip, were being treated: all three had been associated with the strip for over a decade, and now it was being sidelined, reduced to a page and a half. But it looks to the casual observer as though they had simply run out of steam.

This was the thin end of the wedge. On 10 March

1962 the cover changed again. The editorial team were rearranging the deckchairs on the *Titanic*, desperately trying to find a solution to declining sales. In its heyday the *Eagle* was regularly selling 750,000 copies a week, but by the early 1960s the figure was well below 500,000: still healthy but moving in the wrong direction. There were more strip-based comics coming on to the market, and also magazines catering to the various other areas that the *Eagle* covered. One of the things that had made the *Eagle* stand out was that it was never just about the strips. It had text stories, sport, history and much more, but while this made it a market leader in the 1950s, now the market was becoming more specialised. If you were into music you would buy a specialist music magazine, not the *Eagle* with its few music articles; and likewise for sport, adventure and so on.

Another part of the problem for the *Eagle* was that the world had changed. The *Eagle* built its fan base on great British values, which had come to a head during the war with the 'spirit of the Blitz' and the 'fight them on the beaches' attitude. It was us against the world, for the good of the world. At the end of 1962 the Cold War had its scariest moment with the Cuban Missile Crisis, which forced the world to look for détente rather than the hostilities that had been ongoing since before the Second World War. This shift in focus, and the general liberalisation of attitudes symbolised by the period's counterculture, a kick against the values of the 1940s and 1950s, meant that while the solid, homely values of the *Eagle* were still important, they were not necessarily important to the readers of comics.

In 'The Big City Caper', for example, Dan has to tackle indolent London teenagers, who are easily led by Xel in attacking the system. The tone of the story is very disapproving of teen culture, and while its inclusion may have been intended to keep those teens on board, their treatment was very much a turn-off.

On 10 March 1962 *Eagle* appeared for the first time without a Dan Dare story on the cover. There was a trailer for that week's tale, 'Operation Earthsaver', but it hid a dark secret. The frame on the cover was in colour, but when the reader turned to page 6, it can only be hoped they were sitting down because here was 'Dan Dare' in black and white. For this new regime there was a new artist, Keith Watson, and a fresh writer, David Motton.

Eric Eden put down his pen and picked up his brushes and followed where many previous Eaglers had gone before and worked for *TV Century 21*, an offshoot of the Gerry Anderson empire. Thus he worked on many iconic characters who were best known from television. These included Lady Penelope and the rest of the Thunderbirds crew, and Fireball XL5. He was joined there by Don Harley. Don and Bruce Cornwell, both now in their eighties, are still drawing and painting. Much of their work consists of commissions for 'Dan Dare' fans who want their favourite frames recreated.

Keith Watson was the sole artist working on the strip. Colouring in takes a long time, and that was no longer needed. Watson had no formal training as an artist: he began as a fan of the *Eagle* and Dan Dare. Born in 1935, he was fifteen years old when the comic was launched and he was hooked immediately. Once he felt confident enough he speculatively applied for a job by drawing a spoof front cover of the comic. Eventually he was taken on as an assistant artist in 1958, and even stayed on for a short time after Frank Hampson's departure, but left in 1959, going to work for *Lion*, drawing 'Captain Condor', that comic's equivalent of 'Dan Dare'. When the chance came to draw the leading strip in the country he couldn't turn it down, but maybe he didn't realise that it was no longer to be the cover star. For almost the whole of 1963 the cover was filled by a series called 'Kings of the Road', which ostensibly featured famous racing drivers but was actually just an excuse for some great colour art of racing cars.

Watson had been inspired to draw by the early *Eagle*, and during his tenure he did much to restore what he felt were the essential elements of the strip. He wasn't able to bring back Flamer and Peabody, but O'Malley did return every now and then. As a Hampson disciple he was not beyond giving a nod to his hero. The most obvious of these was the reissuing of the Space Fleet uniforms from the early days. Bellamy's New Romantic look was ditched, and it was back to the future. He hadn't been able to bring back Peabody but on the cover for the first episode of 'The Big City Caper' he sneaked her in along with Hank and Pierre, in the cheering crowds who welcome Dan and Digby home. In spite of the limitations of working in black and white, and working alone, Watson did much to restore the reputation of 'Dan Dare' and keep the flame burning.

The loss of colour was obviously noted by the readership, and even though the regular letters page had disappeared, when it did occasionally reappear there were demands that Dan be given his lustre back. Finally, in 1963, a letter from across the pond persuaded the powers that be to give in. 'Dan Dare' fans have Douglas Marden from Hoboken, New Jersey, to thank. His letter was published on 16 March, a full year after Dan had lost his colour. He'd been a reader for ten years, so he said, and 'the best thing that ever appeared on the front page was the Dan Dare feature. The futuristic scenes were never displayed better and I would laud any attempts to return him to the front page in colour.' They used to say that if America sneezed the UK caught a cold, and so who were the men of Fleet Street to argue with the eloquent young Marden? The letter from the editor was no longer signed, which in itself speaks volumes, but a week later a reply came from an anonymous person in the editor's office.

Last week I published the letter from an American reader who said how much he missed Dan Dare in colour on the front page. His was not the only letter I have had expressing the same opinion. In fact, I've had scores. Well, my aim is to give you what you want. So when Dan Dare and Digby step out on the planet Meit next week, their adventures will be recorded on the front page in colour. I'm sure this will mean double enjoyment.

Meit was the planet that Dan and Digby, with a new bunch of colleagues, had arrived at in 'Operation Time Trap'. This was Watson and Motton's sixth adventure, and now they really had hit their stride. The previous tales had involved some interesting creations, such as the deadly cotton-wool-like clouds in 'Web of Fear', the destructive rolling inferno in 'Operation Fireball' and the black-sheep pilot Captain Egon in 'Operation Dark Star', but like the stories of the Eden-Harley-Cornwell era these had often flattered to deceive. Watson's artwork was variable throughout his tenure, ranging from the brilliant to the rushed, but when he got his colours back he produced some beautiful work. He never really managed the intricate detail so important to Hampson, and he didn't have Bellamy's eye for action, but he found his own style and brought the strip into the 1960s with some success.

The narrative arc that began with 'Time Trap' showed ambitions that had not been seen since 'Safari in Space', and produced a tale that ran over six separate stories and two years, ending with 'The Moonsleepers'. Considering there were just the two men working on it, this was a great achievement, and it is this run of work that has given Watson in particular a warm place in the affections of even the most diehard Hampsonite. The narrative innovation of Motton and Watson was to have two competing villains running throughout this period. The Mekon was known to all and the reader knew pretty much what to expect, while Xel, whose catchphrase was 'I am the one who must be obeyed, the one in one thousand million,' came from the Svalokin Empire of Stoll and was the new evil kid on the block.

'Kid' is the operative word here,because his behaviour is like that of a child. He has the strength of a hundred men packed into his small frame, but no patience, no strategic ability; he acts purely on impulse. He is the total opposite of the Mekon. For the reader, who had always thought Dan Dare the total opposite of the Mekon, a dilemma presented itself. Xel and the Mekon confronted each other, then teamed up to confront Dan, and so Dan found himself having to side with one or other of his enemies to defeat the odd-one-out. It made the universe a complicated place, and again reflected the situation in the real world as our wartime allies became our peace-time enemies, and vice versa.

As well this double-enemy scenario, Watson and Motton were also responsible for introducing another member of Dan's family. Nigel Dare, Dan's nephew, turns up briefly in 'The Big City Caper' as one of the teens whom Xel rounds up in his troublemaking team. This actually implies two further members of the family, since Nigel's surname is 'Dare' and we can only assume therefore that Dan has a brother, and probably a sister-in-law. At the end of the 'Caper' Dan decides to set up a commune on a far-off planet as a place where teenagers can be sent to make their own decisions and learn how to live their lives. It can only be assumed that he persuaded Nigel to go there in the first group.

This run of adventures has another theme that relates very much to the times. It had been seen before but here, especially in 'Big City Caper' and 'All Treens Must Die', there is an emphasis on the dangers of mind-altering drugs. In 'Caper' Xel uses a strange transmission to get the teens on his side, and in 'All Treens' the Mekon also uses a brain wave to persuade the Treens to commit suicide. The 1960s saw a massive increase in the use of recreational drugs, giving the government the problem of a proportion of the population being literally out of their minds. Was this the *Eagle*'s subtle attempt to warn children about the dangers of LSD? After all, from the very start Marcus Morris had wanted the magazine to be educational.

All comics were feeling the pinch throughout the decade, not fighting for new readers so much as trying to steal each other's. The situation has similarities with the mobile-phone market in the early twenty-first century, with no new users and the only way to stay in business being to steal them off one's competitors. One obvious method of doing this was to buy up a fading rival while it still had some readers and merge it with your own comic. This was most easily done by merging comics within your own publishing house, leading to certain economies of scale, but the two readerships never add up to the total of those who read both before the merger. What inevitably happens is that first you lose some of the readers of the comic that has been incorporated into a more successful one, and then you lose readers of that magazine too, as they are dissatisfied with the elements from the newcomer that have pushed out some of their favourite items. In the end nobody wins.

With television ownership on the increase, pop music on the rise, and generally more ways for children to spend their pocket money, the marketplace was getting tougher and tougher. Once Odhams had tried incorporating its own comics into the *Eagle* there was only one option left: merger. In 1963 Odhams was brought together with Newnes and Fleetway, formerly Amalgamated Press, to form the International Publishing Corporation (IPC).

This meant that there seemed to be a lot of different products on the market, but they were all now produced by one company, much like washing powders. Further economies of scale were possible, but the downside was homogeneity across the output.

Watson and Motton's work on 'Dare' was sufficiently strong to keep Dan on the cover until 24 July 1965 and the first instalment of 'The Singing Scourge', the first post-Xel/Mekon tale. From the following week Dan was moved to the middle pages. The strip was still in full colour and offered a double-page spread until the end of 'Give Me the Moon', a strange tale where the villain seems to be a blind, mild-mannered janitor, Benny Clark, in fact a disguise used by Laslo Romanov, the son of the world's wealthiest industrialist.

For Watson and Motton's final outing, 'Dan Dare' was reduced to a single inside colour page. By this stage, the content was indistinguishable across the whole range of IPC's products. You could have moved strips from one comic to another and no one would have really noticed, as each comic no longer had its distinct character. The editorial team seemed to have no idea what was good and what wasn't, and this is illustrated by the fact that Frank Bellamy's award-winning 'Heros the Spartan' suffered the same fate as Dan.

When the 'Menace from Jupiter' was brought under control by Dan and Digby, it was in effect their last outing. In Volume 18, no. 1, on 7 January 1967, like an out-of-favour football manager, Dan was kicked upstairs to a quiet office where he wouldn't bother anyone.

Keith Watson's final frame shows Sir Hubert Guest

congratulating Dan on being appointed Controller of Space Fleet. There are a lot of faces from Dan's past in the audience who maybe think this heralds an exciting new time for the old boy. After all, Sir Hubert himself had not allowed his role to stop him gallivanting all over the galaxy. But for Dan it is a retirement of sorts. Rather than continuing to save the world from his new position, he is going to share his wisdom by reproducing his tales of derring-do. The caption announces: *It is intended that the completed manual shall be presented to every space cadet as he begins his training.*

And so for the next two years poorly reproduced and disastrously cut and edited versions of some of the greatest comic work ever was passed off as quality fare for the late-1960s comic buyer. Flicking through these reprints is reminiscent of returning to a childhood home. You have wonderful memories of events that happened there, moments that shaped your life and who you have become. As you drive along the road you see the house in the distance and for a moment you convince yourself that it has not changed, it is the house you grew up in. But on closer inspection you notice the changes: the apple tree that you used to climb has gone, the grass in the front garden has been concreted over and you can never again play cricket on a strip that was, in your youthful mind, better than Lords. Reading these chopped-up versions of 'Prisoners of Space' and then a tragically truncated 'Man from Nowhere' and 'Rogue Planet' is just plain depressing. In the midst of these reprints was a short, flimsy new Dan Dare adventure drawn by Eric Kincaid and called 'Underwater Attack'. This tale has the undeserved kudos of being the last original output of 'Dan Dare' material to appear in the *Eagle*. The artwork itself was technically fine, but it was a pale shadow of Frank Hampson's gloriously detailed vision. Kinaid went on to draw illustrations for classic children's stories such as *The Wind in the Willows* and his work is still much in demand today, but this was a depressing final chapter for the Pilot of the Future.

Frank Hampson had very firm views on the decline of the paper he had created. 'It was always a very expensive paper to produce and I think that's one reason why the opposition wanted to buy it and then kill [it]. With the *Eagle* out of the way, and they killed it pretty soon, the audience was wide open for them. This is the way they do it. Don't kill it dead straight away; they amalgamate the thing.'

The lights finally went out at *Eagle* on 26 April 1969, when it became no more than an addendum to *Lion*. Nineteen years after bursting on to the scene *Eagle* and Dan Dare edged out of the back door, feeling like unwanted guests at someone else's party, hoping no one would notice they were gone.

They could not have been more wrong.

CHAPTER SIX

He Touched
All Our Lives

WHEN *Eagle* disappeared into the *Lion*'s den, taking
Dan, Digby and *Anastasia* with it, there was no reason
to expect the flame to keep burning. The *Eagle* itself had
'incorporated' various publications over the years, such
as *Merry-Go-Round* and *Boy's World*, only for them to
disappear from the masthead when their original readers
stopped caring. *Lion*, which had been launched in 1952
by Amalgamated Press as a direct competitor to *Eagle*,
already had its own version of Dan Dare in the shape
of Captain Condor. As *Eagle* had already lost faith in
Dan, it seemed unlikely that the transfer would reig-
nite any interest in new stories. The worst fears were
realised when *Lion* continued with one more rerun, 'The
Phantom Fleet', and then that was it: Dan was gone from
the pages of British comics.

But, as the Mekon found over their decades of battling,
Daniel McGregor Dare does not give up that easily, and
he just wouldn't go away. The character had been too

robustly created all those years ago on Frank Hampson's kitchen table.

2000 AD was the first comic to use Dan to add some lustre to its appeal. It was launched on 26 February 1977 by IPC, who still owned the rights to Dan Dare and now decided to revive him. Rather than being left to cope in a future created in the distant past, Dan was woken from a two-hundred-year cryogenic sleep. In the *2000 AD* version Dan looks like a pumped-up Clint Eastwood and eventually receives an artificial appendage to his hand, Eternicus, 'the Cosmic Claw'. While this reincarnation was not particularly popular with the diehards – after all they were in their forties and fifties by now – it did bring him back to the public's attention and, somewhat perversely, showed how good the original was. In fact, it was this version that brought Dan to the attention of Nev Fountain, best known for co-creating the BBC comedy sketch show *Dead Ringers* and now a writer for the *Doctor Who* spin-off comic strip and a series of science-fiction novels. Once Nev started reading about Dan in *2000 AD*, his father nipped up to the attic and brought down his copies of the original. This was a familiar route back to the beginning for many.

In *2000 AD* Dan was vying for readers with the newly created Judge Dredd, initially winning the battle as the centre-spread star but eventually giving way. Dan lasted for two years in the comic and, although, at first, he was drawn by the Italian artist Massimo Belardinelli, after six months the task was handed over to Dave Gibbons, who stayed on it till the end. Gibbons is best known now for his work on *The Watchmen*, which finally made it to the cinema screen in 2009, just twenty-three years after its publication as a twelve-part series in 1986. It is well known that Gibbons is a big admirer of Frank Hampson's work, and so drawing Dan was a labour of love. He even met Hampson while working on the strip and apologised for not being able to live up to the original. The thing he was most impressed by was the consistency and, while it is something he strives for in his work, he acknowledged the benefits of the studio system.

Dan was called back to his true home when *Eagle* was relaunched in 1982 with the catchy name *New Eagle*. It wasn't actually Dan, but his great-great-grandson, fighting against the still-going-strong Mekon. The first story begins with the Mekon returning to Earth in search of Dan but finding a grave marked DAN DARE, TEST PILOT – LOST IN ACTION 1950. The Mekon takes this to mean he is dead. *New Eagle*'s idea was that Dan was supposedly a Second World War pilot who became a test pilot after the war, presumed 'lost in action' but in fact the victim of a freak accident in space that threw him forward in time to 1994, where the original *Eagle* placed stories.

This is an interesting example of revisionism but ignores the fact that the Mekon knows Dan did not die in 1950 since he had his various encounters with him in the late twentieth and early twenty-first centuries. *New Eagle* lasted till 1992, and Dan with it. Yet another generation of comic readers were now aware of the name and keen to seek out his history.

With *Spaceship Away*, the excellent quarterly launched in 2003 by Rod Barzilay, Dan inhabits what is essentially a fanzine that manages at the same time to be a tribute to the original 'Dan Dare' strips and also a creator of new adventures. In the first issue Keith Watson provides the art to Barzilay's script for 'The Phoenix Mission', and thus begins a brand-new Dan Dare adventure almost forty years after he finished working on him in the *Eagle*. The project was driven and paid for by fans, but has since become a widely read magazine, bringing in yet another whole new readership. The amazing thing is that 'Phoenix' had been over a decade in the making. Keith Watson, commissioned by Barzilay to draw and advise on the strip, had only got as far as producing the first page when he was diagnosed with cancer. Tragically he died in 1994, aged just fifty-nine. 'The Phoenix Mission', a great title on more than one level, could well have died with him, but Dan Dare continually defies normal logic. Page 2 and subsequent pages are drawn by the ever-reliable Don Harley, and so Dare lives again.

As this shows, it is often the fans more than corporations or publishing houses that keep the ship afloat. As early as the 1960s there were fan clubs determined that Dan should not be lost to the world. The Astral Group was the first, and spent many years trying to persuade Frank Hampson, through personal letters, back to his drawing board. The Astral Group evolved into the Eagle Society, which has been running since the late 1980s and produces a quarterly journal, the *Eagle Times*, which celebrates the original comic and its readers.

One of the mainstays of the society, an original member of the Astral Group, is Adrian Perkins. From external appearances, Adrian Perkins is no different from any other retired man in his mid-sixties. He lives with his wife in a quiet suburb of Cambridge. When he comes to the door you are warmly welcomed by a cheery chap who quickly offers a cup of tea and a biscuit. But Adrian hides an exciting secret. In the back room of his cosy, tidy home is a treasure trove the like of which you will not find in many places. Stacked up on neat shelves in chronological or alphabetical order, depending on which is most appropriate, is everything ever published by Frank Hampson, and anything in print linked to Dan Dare.

Adrian did not go down to his local newsagent's on 14 April 1950, but don't imagine for one minute that this means he did not become an early devotee of the *Eagle*. He was introduced to the world of Dan Dare, Tommy Walls and Professor Brittain by his grandfather, a retired headmaster, who brought the first issue round. True to his roots in the education system, he was not satisfied to just bring this joy into his young relative's world; before delivering no. 1 he spent time going through and making notes in the margins of any words that he thought the lad would not understand. He may have been the first, but he was certainly not the last teacher to recognise the educational benefits of the comic.

Now, sixty years later, Adrian still talks about his collection with the enthusiasm and excitement of a young boy – and this is a young boy who knows his onions. As well as every comic from 14 April 1950 through to 26 April 1969, he has examples of nearly everything that Frank Hampson ever drew, from those early line sketches for *Meccano Magazine*, through his time with *The Post*, and even (though he is not happy with the reproduction) a copy of the winning poster that Frank drew for the Southport Tourist Board. This is a shrine to all things Hampson, and it is a credit to both the owner and the subject.

The highlight here has to be the Presso-produced pop-up book, *Dan Dare, Pilot of the Future*. It is filed under P for 'Presso', but that could also be for 'pristine' as the colours are as vibrant as they were on the day in 1953 when the book was published. The pop-up scenes are works of art, both in the drawing and in the paper craftsmanship. Most of Adrian's collection can be found in the British Library at King's Cross and the national newspaper collection in Colindale, but there are three things that make a visit to the outskirts of Cambridge more rewarding, if you are lucky enough to get the invite. First, Adrian's collection is complete, unlike the British Library's, and second, he can find things faster with his system, and third, of course, the biscuits are better.

The thing that makes Dare unique is that he seems to have struck a chord with people right across the smorgasbord of British society. Sir Tim Rice is best known for his collaborations with Andrew Lloyd Webber, Elton John and Benny Andersson and Björn Ulvaeus of ABBA, and while he and Adrian Perkins have never collaborated on anything they do share an abiding love of Dan Dare. Sir Tim was born in 1944 and so was slightly too young for the arrival of the *Eagle*, but he was hitting the real target age in the years just before Frank Hampson left. Thanks to his father's prudence, Sir Tim still has the first decade and a half of the comic in mint condition.

He is not 100 per cent sure why Dan has survived so long, but he knows why he was such a fan. Dan is 'a decent chap, honest, brave, good-looking . . . And he's a winner.' It was the good stories that kept young Tim coming back for more, as well as the 'interesting astronomical information'. In an era when the word of the famous is sought on every topic, it appears that Sir Tim has become a spokesman for 'Dan Dare' fans everywhere. He has introduced reproduced collections of the stories, as well as writing the foreword for *Living with Eagles*.

Interestingly his favourite stories are not from what is generally regarded as the golden age, but instead he has a penchant for the Venus story and 'Operation Saturn'. This probably explains why his favourite characters are the original crew and his feeling that the later characters never quite lived up to them. Like most readers looking back at the comic, he confesses unprompted to finding Peabody sexy.

It was on the eve of the 2010 general election when Sir Tim gave his views on *Eagle* for this book, and he had a message to the potential victor of that election: 'Don't trust green blokes.' Ecologically minded voters and politicians, especially those in Brighton, should not take offence; he was of course referring to the Mekon.

Less well known to the man on the street but producing work that is read by comic fans the world over and watched by devotees of BBC TV's *Doctor Who* is writer Paul Cornell. Cornell's 'character as a writer was formed in the moment I cracked open those crates of *Eagle Annuals*, Enid Blyton, Biggles, *Galaxy* and *Worlds of If*. The crates he refers to are those of his older brother, which were left when he moved to Australia. Cornell is rather too young to have been around when the *Eagle* first hit the streets and so he only came across Dan Dare and co., as well as many other iconic characters, when going through the childhood reading of his departed brother. The influence of those comics and specifically Dan Dare on his writing is further shown when he writes that 'Prof. Peabody is a wonderful Commonwealth-era attempt at first feminism, and her DNA is in all my heroines.'

As for why Dan is such an enduring character, he goes on to say, 'I think that he's weirdly forward-looking, while being entirely British. He keeps going like that space future for us was true. It's the central British alternate reality. He plays by the rules. That's one of the things I love about him. I doubt his world government had the death penalty. And the fact that he does kill, but only when he really has to, is the absolute best thing about the stories, the perfect balance.'

Many of Frank Hampson's theories about space travel have come true, if not to the extent that he expected. Advances in communications also showed Dan using the videophone, both at the office and on the move. Also in 'Voyage to Venus' was the *Ranger* spaceship, which carried the three smaller ships to the edge of Venus. The NASA space shuttle programme did not actually come into operation until 1981, though they had been looking into it since the late 1960s. Did someone at NASA have an old copy of the *Eagle*? Cornell looks at the world created by the strip in a slightly different light: 'I was really hoping for that space Olympics, but Dan's world isn't about pure prediction. There's also an inbuilt satire. There's a lot of Heath Robinson or a British *Jetsons* in the depictions of, for instance, Digby's auntie's cottage. The world's built really well, but there's also the capacity for a knowing self-mockery, of just the right measure, in there.'

Cornell reveres Frank's work: 'I'd say the Hampson issues are in the league of best strip anywhere. I love the way "The Man from Nowhere" segues into "Reign of the Robots". There are the two big SF stories: interstellar mission and Earth invaded, back to back. I see good work [in those that followed him], but even Bellamy doesn't approach Hampson for me. It's the design of the world, the faces, and the money spent on studio time and assistance.' Coming from a writer of some of the twenty-first century's most popular comics and television programmes, that is praise indeed. And when Cornell is in doubt about what he should do, which course he should take when times are tough, 'Myself, I try and ask, what would Dan do?'

Another writer heavily influenced by the *Eagle*, 'Dan Dare' and Frank Hampson is Chris Claremont, best known for his work on 'The X-Men'. His grandmother paid for a subscription to the comic all through his youth; he lived in the States from the age of three and she sent it over. Although he read *Batman* and *Superman*, the *Eagle* was more exciting because it mingled science fiction with 'proper' fiction. He carried on reading the comic when Hampson made 'The Road of Courage', and was enthralled by the way the son of God was portrayed as just a normal kid. It was only later, looking back at the strip, that he noticed how similar Jesus looked to Dan Dare!

Claremont's career got going just as the *Eagle* was finishing, when he got a job as office runner at Marvel Comics. Within five years he was given his own strip to write, 'Iron Fist', and just a year later he was paired with John Byrne, another Hampsonite, for 'X-Men'.

As writers of comic strips rather than artists, it is interesting that both Cornwell and Claremont cite Hampson as a major influence, because, while most people think of Hampson as a brilliant artist, he always believed that the most important thing was to tell the story. The art was a means to an end, not the end itself.

Frank refers to this in an article he wrote for the *World's Press News and Advertiser's Review* in December 1951. His contribution is prefaced by a two-page article about the growth of children's comics in the UK. It was indicative of comics' growing importance that one of the country's leading industry papers was devoting space to them. The article looked at three stages of the comic, of which the third, referred to as the 'New Age of Comics', was *Eagle* and its sister paper *Girl*.

Frank writes of 'continuity', referring to the fact that one must assume that a reader will read each strip twice: once for the actual story and once again to scrutinise the details. These details give depth and realism to the story. Because of this double read it is important to change the viewpoint so that not all frames look the same. The final element is draughtsmanship, and this relates to the flow of the story. In an ideal world, he explains, one should be able to follow the story without reading the speech bubbles.

Another artist influenced by Hampson is Bryan Talbot, who has worked on 'Batman', 'Judge Dredd', 'Sandman' and many more. Referring to his comic-book series about sexual abuse, *The Tale of One Bad Rat*, he says that Frank's 'influence on my Bad Rat artwork was the strong ink outline with texture and shading done using colour, and his extensive use of photo ref to add verisimilitude to his drawings'.

He went on to say:

I was born and raised in Wigan during the 1950s, not twenty miles from where Hampson and his team were producing Dan Dare, but of course didn't realise it at the time. The *Eagle* was a very middle-class publication and I think that's why I never read it while I was growing up. In fact, I only read the more 'serious' comics like the *Valiant* and the *Lion* occasionally, at friends' houses. I preferred the DC Thomson funny comics. But once, when I was about seven or eight, we drove what seemed to me a vast distance (about a hundred miles) to visit one of my dad's brothers' family for the weekend, and my cousins had an *Eagle* annual. I vividly remember reading 'Dan Dare' there for the first time and marvelling at the wonderful artwork. When the reprints began to appear in the 1970s I started collecting them. The artwork, with its extensive use of photo ref, was one of the influences on my choice of artwork style for *The Tale of One Bad Rat*. I've done cover illustrations of Dan Dare twice, most recently for the first cover of the Garth Ennis Virgin series.

His final reason for falling for the strip is that 'Of course, Digby also came from Wigan!'

Talbot's comment about the *Eagle* being a middle-class comic is interesting and is borne out by what other people have said. In Terry Jones's house they had never been allowed a comic before, and it was only by convincing his father that the *Eagle* had educational content that the future Python and his older brother were allowed to buy it. Even then it was kept in a drawer, in case any of the neighbours saw it. Sales, though, could not have been as high as they were if it was confined to the middle classes. It was bought by working-class households because it was seen as aspirational: if your kids read it they would get on. It wasn't just full of funnies, like a lot of the competition.

It wasn't easy to persuade his father to let them have the *Eagle* at all:

> I can remember when we first bought the *Eagle*, my mother – because that was in the days when comics were really disapproved of – my mother bought it for my brother and we had to hide it in the kitchen drawer and sort of approach it gently with Dad that we'd bought a comic. We sold it to Dad on 'This man's a vicar.' Then he approved of it and so we got it every week.

This was a tough sell:

> I remember my dad being very severe because he'd grown up in Edwardian England and felt he should be the authority figure and lay down the law. You couldn't put your elbows on the table, you had to chew everything forty-five times, and all that kind of stuff. My father arriving back [after the war] gave me a feeling of what the Edwardian era was like and the *Eagle* arriving was part

of exploding that world, when you didn't have to read literature; comics could be a perfectly viable art form.

Jones's description of his father's return after the war recalls the lack of male influences on wartime children and how Dan filled a gap for those whose fathers didn't return.

It was our first Christmas in Claygate. We'd moved down because my dad had come back from the war in 1946. I was four and a half and he'd been out in India so I'd never seen him, I'd never met him. I remember meeting him at the railway station and Mum getting terribly worried that he was not on [the train] and then at the end of the platform there was this guy in a forage cap, kitbag, and he kisses my mum and he kisses my brother, and then he picks me up and kisses me and, aargh, he's got a moustache. Terribly prickly moustache. I'd never been kissed by anyone with a moustache. I was used to women.

The memories of his father's moustache on his cheek take him back to that time and reading 'Dan Dare', and all the elements that made it special come tumbling out.

I thought the story was brilliant. The great twist where they're captured by the Mekon and Digby comes up trumps by getting the message back to *Anastasia* about the holiday in Cleethorpes. That's great that he came up trumps. The characters are great; Miss Peabody, even the reaction to Miss Peabody, which seems dated now but at the time was interesting, and the gradual discovery of the planet.

The wonderful Theron passivity, and Dan waking up in the Theron household. The invention, and Hampson's detail of the vegetation, of the creatures, that little stripy creature with the elephant's nose, just breathtaking. I thought *Avatar* took a lot from Hampson. The design of the world in *Avatar*, I thought, This is Hampson.

David Preece grew up on the Aspley council estate in Nottingham in the 1940s and his father was a little easier to persuade into allowing the *Eagle* into the house.

My father was a colliery blacksmith, my mother didn't work, she looked after us, myself and my two sisters, so there wasn't a lot of cash going round. We lived fairly reasonably inside certain parameters. I used to get comics from [the newsagents] that were imported from the States. My dad frowned on these so I used to hide them in an old shoebox. [But the *Eagle* was different.] In many ways it was a Christian-type comic even though there was violence and skulduggery, it was done with a very straightforward, very clean, Christian attitude. The teachers at school, my teacher at Sunday school, knew about the *Eagle*, and were all quite encouraging about it. My brother-in-law, who is about nine years older than me, he was a teacher and he remembers using the cutaways as a teaching aid.

Having already been a reader of UK comics such as *Radio Fun* and *Film Fun*, *Beano*, *Dandy*, the coming of the *Eagle* was a momentous occasion.

School kids were talking about it. I knew it was coming out on the Friday and I normally went there [the newsagents] on that day. It was a small shop, forty-five minutes walk away from my home, owned by a lady called Mrs Cook. She was quite middle-aged, about sixty, and kept this shop that sold all sorts of magazines and a whole range of comics. [At 3d.] It was more expensive, some comics at that time were a ha'penny or a penny. This was quite a hike particularly to me as an ordinary person from an ordinary working-class background. A lot of people shared it. I remember people swapping comics at school. Many arguments would break out with kids going; 'Look I've given you two weeks' *Eagle* and I've only had one *Film Fun* from you.'

Not every family could afford it. [But] It was amazing. Even to feel it, not only the format, which was much larger than an ordinary comic was then, but the actual quality of the paper, the smoothness of the paper, it wasn't the rough paper that you'd get in *Radio Fun*. It had got such a variety of things that did interest me. Obviously on the front cover, 'The Pilot of the Future – Dan Dare'. Those stories were so mind-blowing to me. That you could just fly off in a spaceship to Venus and meet and be harassed by the Treens and the Mekon. It was absolutely explosive in your mind. I can remember thinking back to when I first started to read the *Eagle*, it was all in the future, you thought, wow, could this really happen. It was just terrific. All of the colour illustration was really really good. There was some class distinction but it didn't upset me or I wasn't really aware of it at that age. It's quite obvious that there were different strata of society. I always regretted that I couldn't go to the Festival of Britain in 1951. I [remember] they talked a lot about that in the *Eagle*. And I remember my dad, after I'd implored him endless times, he said, No, we can't afford it. We can't go at the weekend because I'll be working overtime and we *can not* afford it, David.' Seeing bits about it in the *Eagle*, reading letters from people that had been, or reports of some fantastic thing that they'd seen there, there was always a pang of regret. There still is. If there's one in 2051, I'll be 110 years old, so it's unlikely. I can't remember anybody at our school going to it either [but] it was important to keep reading the *Eagle* every week.

Frank's approach to comic-strip-drawing makes it very similar to film or television production, and it is no coincidence that there is a crossover between comic-strip artists and storyboard artists. It is also no coincidence that film has been greatly influenced by Dan Dare, Hampson and his team, not just in terms of the visual style but also the technology and the worlds he created. Jones really appreciates this element of the strip: 'I just thought he was a genius. You've got these different shots and angles. It's very obviously filmic. The [close-up of a] traffic light and the ship taking off [in the background], he was lighting it from a film point of view. He was thinking in film and subconsciously it must have gone in. He was a genius, bloody amazing. I kick myself that I never met him.' Jones had the chance to meet Frank in the 1970s when he was producing a book with fellow Python Michael Palin. 'Mike and I did a thing called *Dr Fegg's Encyclopaedia of All World Knowledge*, and we wanted Frank Hampson to do a page but we were persuaded out of it and I really regret it. Actually Frank Bellamy did a really wonderful job for us, but I really would like to have at least met Hampson.'

Just pick up any Dan Dare story, flick through it at random and as sure as Digby is Wigan's finest you will see something that has been used somewhere else since. It would be impossible to go through every reference, but here are some of the best examples of people who could have been influenced by the Pilot of the Future.

Let's start with the creator of one of the biggest TV (and now film) franchises in the world: *Star Trek*. One of the pieces of technology that most caught the viewers' imaginations was the teleporter. The cry of 'Beam me up, Scotty!' has become a catchphrase in its own right used by people who are not remotely fans of it. Devotees of the show and its various iterations will know that it was created by Gene Roddenberry. Like Frank Hampson he served in the Second World War, but unlike Frank he did manage to get into the air force. When hostilities were over he was a commercial pilot for a while before joining the police and finally settling on a life as a writer. The first *Star Trek* series only ran from 1966 to 1969, when it was cancelled due to falling audiences. Like many brilliant creations, its worth was only realised after it had gone. The teleporter, with its trademark sound and light effects, was one of the core 'tricks' of the show. Hampson beat him to it, of course. In 'Voyage to Venus' the Treens use their 'telesender' to get quickly from place to place. It is explained quite succinctly when it first appears on 11 August 1950: 'Don't be afraid of the telesender, Spaceman – you will simply be disintegrated in that cabinet, transmitted by radio and reassembled in a similar cabinet . . .'

This introduced a running joke for the next fifteen years, whereby Digby would always arrive upside down at the other end in spite of his plea for his wires not to get crossed. Frank Hampson obviously noticed the compliment paid him by *Star Trek*. 'Well, they really cleaned out "Dan Dare" in *Star Trek* . . . I had a great admiration for Mr Spock. His role was very much like that of Sondar in my stories, a person with little or no emotions, a kind of steadying influence on the poor humans!' The other similarity, of course, was that both Spock and Sondar turned their backs on their own people.

The first panel of the 17 August 1956 *Eagle* shows a huge spherical satellite flying through the blackest of space. It looks not dissimilar to the *Death Star* from George Lucas's *Star Wars*. While the *Death Star* is a satellite reputed to be able to destroy a whole planet in one go, the *Kra* is ostensibly a refugee ship but it hides a much darker secret. In 'Rogue Planet' it carries a whole generation of Crypts, their teachers, animals and plants from the planet. It journeys for a thousand years before returning the descendants of those who boarded it to rebuild their civilisation after it has once again been destroyed by the Phants.

Just over a year later, on 6 December 1957, the first panel has another forerunner of the *Death Star*, and this one is if anything even more closer to Lucas's model. In 'Reign of the Robots' the Mekon uses a secret satellite to transmit his orders to his army of Elektrobots. Not as direct a weapon as the *Death Star*, but just as destructive.

FOUR ARTISTS

DAN DARE

HAMPSON

THEN, BY GOLLY, WE'LL DISTURB 'EM! I KNOW THE VERY THING . . . .

BELLAMY

DIG, 'FLAMER' - GET BACK TO ANASTASIA, PREPARE THE DISINTEGRON PROJECTOR IN THE MOBILE FRONT SECTION, DRIVE BACK HERE AND PICK UP MY TRAIL. I'M GOING AHEAD — ALONE!

HARLEY

AM CUTTING IN VERNIERS FOUR AND FIVE TO CORRECT!

WATSON

Frank Hampson created Dan Dare, his world and the people in it. When he left, the job was handed to Frank Bellamy, then Don Harley and finally Keith Watson. Each artist brought something unique to the work and this section shows how their styles compare.

HAMPSON

BELLAMY

HARLEY

WATSON

DIGBY

HAMPSON

BELLAMY

HARLEY

WATSON

FLAMER

HAMPSON

BELLAMY

HARLEY

GUEST

HAMPSON

BELLAMY

HARLEY

WATSON

FOUR ARTISTS

MEKON

HAMPSON

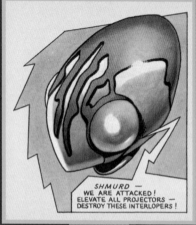

BELLAMY

HARLEY

WATSON

Frank Bellamy never drew The Mekon so this page
includes an equally nasty type from his brush.

O'MALLEY

HAMPSON

NOT YET,
YOU SWAB!

BELLAMY

HARLEY

WATSON

HAMPSON

BELLAMY

HARLEY

A third and final sci-fi giant is the *Alien* series. Possibly best remembered for the iconic moment when an infant alien bursts out of John Hurt's stomach, this series of films clearly has echoes of 'Dan Dare'. That baby grows into a hideous monster very quickly, and it is easy to see parallels with Hampson's favourite villain. With an over-sized head and the ability to learn very quickly, the alien has a one-track mind and allows no one to get in its way. By the fourth film we have seen time and again how the Queen breeds and produces an army in her own image, all of whom follow her commands without question, in the same way as the Mekon developed his Treens.

Ridley Scott, director of the first film and with two prequels currently in development, is a well-known fan of the *Eagle*. He was twelve when the first comic hit the streets and while his first feature film, *The Duellists*, was a historical drama, his next three were in line with his youthful reading, as *Blade Runner* and *Legend* followed *Alien*.

Like 'Dan Dare', *Alien* is set in a world where space travel is commonplace. The ship and crew from the first film are on their way back from a routine mining expedition when they are diverted to the SOS that leads to disaster. How many 'Dan Dare' stories began: 'Dan and Digby were on a routine flight . . .'? From the overall design of the ships and their everyday purpose through to the suspended-animation cells that handily keep Ripley and the alien alive for a new generation, there is a similarity to 'Dare'. That first film has at its core 'the Crew', in the same way as Dan has his team around him.

The spaceships in 'Dan Dare', as we have already seen,

were designed with almost as much care as a real flying machine and were both inspired by, and an inspiration for, genuine craft. Frank and the team would work out how they could in theory fly, what the controls would do and how they would be positioned. This level of detail has made the ships a blueprint for almost every fictional spaceship seen since. They created so many that it would be pretty hard to make up something they hadn't devised beforehand. A classic example is *Thunderbirds*. You can take any one of the *Thunderbirds* craft and find an equivalent in 'Dan Dare'. In fact, you can find three of them in just one story: 'Reign of the Robots'.

On 27 December 1957, a red-nosed rocket very much like *Thunderbird 1* is launched from an underground headquarters on Venus. Dare is flying this rocket, with a fusion bomb warhead, to try and destroy the 'death star' satellite. Have a look at the first panel of 3 January 1958 and you will see a whole fleet of *Thunderbird 2*s. It is from these ships that the Mekon launches his mighty forces of Selektrobots. The *MEK1* satellite, whose picture fills the page on 26 April 1957, acts as a holding station for prisoners before they are shipped off to Mekonta. It would appear to be the inspiration for *Thunderbird 5*. They're not direct copies, but you can see where the germs of the ideas came from. If Frank Hampson were still alive he would see touches of his own work here and be proud of it.

Martin Bower started reading the *Eagle* when he was eight years old and has always been influenced by it. He went on to build models for *Thunderbirds*, but also worked on *Space 1999*, *Blake's 7*, *Doctor Who* and *The Tomorrow People*. In film, he worked on the classic *Alien* and the maybe less than classic, but still popular, *Flash Gordon*. He is still kept busy today, making models based on the stories on commissions for fans. While he never did direct copies of Dan Dare for his daily work, he does remember that for '*Flash Gordon* I did a load of spacecraft for a "spaceship graveyard" [*à la* Sargasso Sea of Space in 'Reign of the Robots'], and one ship was straight out of "Dan Dare"!'

Musician Jeff Wayne is another huge 'Dare' fan. Although born in America, Wayne spent four formative years of his childhood (from the ages of nine to thirteen) in north London from 1953. Already a fan of comics from his homeland, Wayne quickly discovered the joys of the British market in both the funnies and the *Eagle*. It was around the same time that he became a big fan of H. G. Wells's science-fiction masterpiece *The War of the Worlds* through *Classics Illustrated*, a comic book that brought the literary greats to a wider market. In under fifty pages it recreated H. G. Wells's work, finishing off with a biography of the man himself and a nudge in the direction of the original book. Just the sort of presentation Marcus Morris would have approved, and Hampson would have been quite impressed with the artwork too.

The War of the Worlds was written in 1898, and shows Earth being invaded by Martians. A particular version of it had a major effect on Frank Hampson.

What had most effect was *The War of the Worlds*, H. G. Wells, which was beautifully illustrated in *The Passing Show*, I think, by Fortunino Matania, who was I think my favourite illustrator. Except that he gets very little character into people's faces, everything else is absolutely superb. Quite representational, so that when he came on to fantasy, like *War of the Worlds*, he was particularly good because the one thing that makes fantasy believable is to make it look as realistic as possible. Not misty things, you want things exactly delineated and then they really are fantastic.

Wayne produced his best-selling concept album based on the book in 1978, and it has become as much a part of his life as ever it was of Wells's. Thirty-two years after it was first released, a live stage show based on the album toured the world, with Wayne conducting. Wayne draws parallels between Wells and Hampson, in their vision of a certain type of future and the use of science fiction to spell out their message. Wayne sees himself on the same continuum, picking up where they left off and taking these great stories around the globe.

Wayne is not the only person in the world of music to have been influenced by Dan Dare. Sir Richard Branson seems to have spent much of his later life trying to emulate the Pilot of the Future. With various tilts at world records from attempting the fastest Atlantic crossing to circumnavigating the globe in a hot-air balloon he has continually pushed himself and his resources to the limits. Throughout all of these adventures he was inspired by the Colonel.

Dan Dare is a heroic, thoughtful and fiercely independent character; I was an avid reader of his epic journeys. [He is] such a legendary character – one of the original great aviators

Branson is joined by another musical knight, Sir Elton John.

Dan Dare was one of my favourite childhood comic characters, and it was an enthusiasm shared by Bernie Taupin and led to our writing "Dan Dare - Pilot of the Future" for the 1975 *Rock of the Westies* album.

Because of when they were born it is no real surprise that these two should be such followers of Dare. (Contemporaries David Bowie and Syd Barrett also refer to Dan dare in their lyrics.) More of a shock is to find David Lewis Gedge, lead singer, song-writer and core of indie-legends The Wedding Present purring over Hampson's work. The first public hint of this was the appearance on the *Lovenest* single in 1991 of an instrumental track named *Dan Dare*. It was, says Gedge now, an attempt to produce 'a theme tune for a Dan Dare TV or radio programme. I wanted it to make you think of a swash-buckling space-travelling hero.' He certainly achieved that with liberal use of the trademark towering *Wedding Present* guitar sound which dips, then soars and thunders along with the speed of *Anastasia* at full-tilt. In the days of the graphic novel it is maybe not such a surprise to find DLG, as he signs himself, reading comics and it was way back as a child that he was first introduced to them.

My dad used to occasionally come home from work with a *Batman* comic for me and I instantly became addicted. I think he later came to regret exposing me to this particular culture because, when we moved abroad, we had an argument about my wanting to take my entire comic collection with me! [My favourite characters were] Batman, Robin and Alfred, obviously . . . but, erm, Catwoman also made quite an impact on a growing lad, of course. I never saw the original *Eagle* comic . . . but I did retrospect-ively collect copies of those wonderful *Eagle* annuals, which is where I first came across Dan Dare. I think it was mainly the intricate artwork. It was always meticulously drawn and incredibly bold and colourful. But I suppose I've also always been partial to science fiction in general and, in particular, the future as it was imagined in the 1950s.

Having also written a song entitled 'Shatner', after William Shatner who played Captain James T. Kirk in *Star Trek*, the obvious question is who would he prefer to have as his pilot on a space voyage.

Colonel Daniel McGregor Dare himself. Doesn't every-body want to save the world and look devilishly handsome doing it? Even his name's perfect, which is why I wanted to use it for the song title. [Also] I might get a little bored. Of. Shatner's. Over. Acting.

So, thanks to his longevity, Dan Dare has now inspired three generations, in fields from art and literature to space travel and science. The list of famous fans is as long as it is broad, from almost all the Pythons – especially Terry Jones and Michael Palin – to Prince Charles. Some of these fans have had the kudos of appearing in the *Eagle*, and one such is the cartoonist and illustrator Gerald Scarfe. Not only did he win one of the competitions for a treasured Ingersoll Dan Dare watch, he also appeared on the prosaically named 'Readers' Efforts' page. His drawing, entitled 'Eagle Artist's Nightmare', shows various characters in the wrong outfits. Interestingly, two years later Frank Hampson produced a strip for the festive edition of 24 December 1954 entitled 'The Editor's Christmas Nightmare'.

Gerald Scarfe's Christmas nightmare

Perhaps it is fitting therefore for the final word to go to one of the world's best-known scientists, Professor Stephen Hawking. Born in 1942, he is probably most famous for attempting to give the man in the street some knowledge of scientific principles in his book *A Brief History of Time*. When he was asked how Dan Dare had influenced him, he simply replied, 'Why am I in cosmology?'

CHAPTER SEVEN

Selling Dan:
The Merchandising of a Pilot
of the Future

ONE OF Frank Hampson's greatest bugbears was that everyone seemed to be making money out of Dan Dare apart from him; but he was equally, if not more, upset that nothing ever went back to the original cause. 'Hultons published it but unfortunately it wasn't any use to the society (SCP) that had originally been the reason for founding it because they took it on on the basis simply of paying off Marcus's debts, taking us on the staff and producing it as a commercial venture. The society rather vanished, I'm afraid.' He, or perhaps Marcus Morris on his behalf, had sold the rights to the characters, the strip and everything to do with it to Hulton Press. It was therefore in Hulton Press's power to make hay for as long as the sun shone – and shine it did, very brightly.

As magazine publishers, the way Hulton made money was to franchise out the rights to the characters to companies who specialised in toys, games, replica clothing and, well, almost anything. A quick search today on eBay will bring up much that is good, and bad, of what was produced under the Dan Dare banner. It is a sign of his enduring popularity that some of these items now fetch a good price. It's also a sign of his popularity at the time that there is so much out there.

These products were sold through the normal outlets for toys and games but, because it had a vested interest in their success, the *Eagle* obviously lent a hand in the marketing. One of the first methods was the '*Eagle* Window', in which a short text advert would offer some quite incredible merchandise. Here are some examples of the weird and the wonderful offered via the '*Eagle* Window':

No. 84: Dan Dare Mercury Bootees – straight from the planet Mercury. And what's more they have rubber soles so can be worn indoors and out. These can only be bought at Dolcis [by coincidence Ruari McLean, who was responsible for *Eagle*'s typeface, also designed the Dolcis shop signs' lettering]; and a word of warning – be quick, they're certain to go like quicksilver.

No. 192: Dan Dare Furnishing Fabric – Space Ships in your den, or Dan on the covers of your bedroom chairs. Made of Spun Rayon with background colours in pale shades of blue, green and fawn. 3/11d. a yard (35" wide).

No. 208: Dan Dare Iced Lollies – Among the very best Iced Lollies are these cleverly moulded to represent Dan Dare. They are refreshing and delicious. The Mekon couldn't lick him but now you can!

As well as these mini-advertorials there were normal adverts offering the whole range of Dare-related items. At times it seemed that the comic was being produced solely to sell Dan Dare paraphernalia. In one issue chosen at random (21 November 1952) I found the following *Eagle* spin-off-related adverts: page 5, Dan Dare belts and braces; page 6b, Jeff Arnold boots, Dan Dare watch, Dan Dare space outfit, *Eagle* tie, *Eagle* film projector, 'Riders of the Range' jersey; page 10a, Dan Dare suit (not to be confused with the space outfit in the earlier advert), Dan Dare watch (*again!*). Maybe that issue was an unfair choice as it was so close to Christmas, but it was a bombardment and must have given parents a real headache.

Possibly one of the most sought-after items now, and at the top of the range in the 1950s, was the Ingersoll Dan Dare pocket watch. If they are still in working order they are very much in demand today, and can fetch over £300. Not bad for an original outlay of thirty shillings. It's a nice piece of work, with the second hand being a spinning Space Fleet badge. Ingersoll knew a good thing when they saw it, and also produced a 'Riders of the Range' version.

As the majority of Dan Dare fans were small boys, it was inevitable that a large number of guns would be produced. Although Marcus Morris had objected to the violence in American comics, he was not in a position to stop the merchandising machine as it churned out guns of all sorts: a Rocket Gun, an Atomic Gun, a Ray Gun, an Aqua Jet Gun, a Cosmic Ray Gun, a Planet Gun, a Space Gun and even the catchily named Space

Projector Gun, which projected pictures from the strips. The boxes for these guns invariably showed Dan firing said gun, even though in the 'Dan Dare' stories violence really was meant to be a last resort.

This last item was one of many projectors that bore Dan's likeness. Merit was the main producer for these projectors, and they weighed in with the Spaceship Film Viewer, which was shaped like a spaceship, modelled on the *Hermes* from 'Marooned on Mercury'. Also in the range was a non-branded projector that came with various different strips as well as 'Dan Dare', such as 'Archie Andrews' and 'Tiger Tim'. This obviously allowed 'Dare' fanatics to have a full show, with the others as the support films. If you just wanted to enjoy these strips by yourself there were also small hand-held film-strip viewers. Was this how Ridley Scott got into filmmaking?

There was much to keep the budding spaceship builder occupied too, thanks mainly to A. & M. Bartram. They produced Airfix-type offerings of both a spaceship and a rocket. These included blueprints for the crafts and a fairly simple construction with nuts and bolts. They wouldn't have flown any further than the average ten-year-old could throw them, but this was not true of the rather ambitious Space Ship Kit powered by the Jetex motor. This motor was the marvel of its day and allowed model makers the world over to get their creations airborne. Although very small, it produced a powerful thrust, using gas in a combustion chamber that was ignited by a wick. In effect it was a sophisticated firework.

Bruce Cornwell recalls just how like a firework it was. One of his jobs in the team was to make models of the various spaceships, in the main to help the artists with scaling, continuity and perspective, and so on. But on one occasion he was asked by Marcus to produce a working model of *Anastasia*. He was excused drawing work for a whole week to build the model out of balsawood, and his engine of choice was the Jetex. A first effort disappeared into the wild blue yonder, but a second was deemed of sufficient quality to show to Marcus. It was quite rare for Marcus to have any direct contact with the artists, and Bruce only recalls seeing him on a couple of occasions, so this encounter sticks in his mind. Sadly it was not an auspicious occasion. Bruce's *Annie* took off OK but never got much height; it flew just off the ground along Marcus's garden, with bits breaking off, before it eventually crashed in the bushes. Marcus burned his fingers trying to retrieve it from the shrubbery and instantly decided it was too dangerous a thing to be sold. In Bruce's memory, 'It wasn't safe for the kiddies so that was the end of it.'

But memory can play tricks on us. Somehow this death trap of a toy did make it into the shops. It was produced by Wilmot Mansour and Co., who were also the developers of the Jetex engine. The pieces of the ship were pre-moulded balsa, and it all seems pretty much as Bruce designed it, with the possible addition of a launch ramp. As the company was quite renowned for this sort of craft, at their peak they were producing 3,000 kits a week, so one has to assume that they made a better job of it than Bruce.

Coincidentally, Wallis Rigby, probably the best-known

maker and designer of paper aeroplanes this country has ever produced, was also an avid user of Jetex engines to power his creations. He first came to prominence with his design for a paper model of the plane that Amy Johnson had flown to Australia. Later he was responsible for the Presso book *Dan Dare's* Anastasia *Jet Plane*. This beautiful book allows the reader to press out the pre-cut pages and put together their own version of *Anastasia*. It is very rare to find a copy now as, of course, most people who bought it did what was expected and made the plane. They hold a copy at the British Library and it is well worth going along to have a look at it. It is a fantastic example of British design and ingenuity. It is tempting to start building the ship there and then, but it is not advised.

Slightly less ambitious was the remote-controlled helicopter set. If 'remote' means being a couple of inches away, connected by a wire, then this lives up to its name. This was essentially a propeller on the end of a stick, attached to a base that was also attached to the remote control. This meant the 'helicopter' could fly in a circle around the base. It seems dull, but it did have three speeds, one of which was reverse. Some readers may recall the Verti-Bird from the 1970s, which was a slightly better version of Dan's 'copter.

Communication was obviously an important part of any spaceman's life, and the franchisees were quick to jump on this bandwagon too. One of the most popular items was the Dan Dare Space Control Radio Station. The box promised that it would be possible to send, and receive, voice and code over as much as half a mile. This would probably contravene legislation on radio transmitters nowadays, but in the 1950s the airwaves were free to all. Pirate radio was first popularised in the UK in the 1960s, but this forerunner would have allowed *Eagle* fans to broadcast their own material ten years before, and they wouldn't have had to do it from a boat in the Channel. The sets were produced by J. & L. Randall of Potters Bar, the company that used 'Merit' as its trading name. They also produced the walkie-talkie set. This sold itself as 'two-way' (what would be the point if it were only one-way?), and proclaimed on the box that 'It really works.' A proud boast indeed, and this was indeed another popular item, especially as it did not require batteries but was instead powered magnetically. It wasn't much more than two tin cans with a connecting piece of string, but if the string was long enough it could be a useful device. Well, that was the theory. The handsets were the same as those used on the radio station and lead one to think that perhaps the boast about sending and receiving up to half a mile relates to the length of the wire.

In the *Dan Dare Space Book*, one of Digby's hobbies is given as 'jigsaw'. *Eagle* fans could join in by buying Dan Dare puzzles. The puzzles were mainly produced by Waddingtons or Theydon; the difference between the two companies was that Waddingtons tended not to use the original artwork, while Theydon did. One of the best jigsaws was of the Venusian Embassy party from the opening of 'The Man from Nowhere'. The puzzles weren't limited to squares and rectangles, as Waddingtons produced some really quite nice circular ones that showed several scenes from individual stories.

Clothing was another popular item, and Dan was certainly a belt-and-braces type of chap if these are anything to go by. As well as the various means of keeping up one's trousers, there were also ties, and indeed whole spaceman's outfits. Before venturing out in his Dan Dare costume, a young pilot would want to make sure his personal hygiene was up to standard and so could use Calvert's Dan Dare tooth powder. With a picture of Dan on the tin, this was the ideal way to make sure the kids kept their pearly-whites in good condition. As further incentive, if that were really needed, each pack contained a picture card. These could be kept for ever in an album which you had to send off for. In the days before Panini monopolised the card-collecting world these were the source of swapsies in the playground.

Pepys, mass producer of card games, of course made a Dan Dare version. They also made a set for *Girl*. Dan's was called Game of the Future and featured forty-four cards split into four sets in red, green, yellow and blue. Each set was numbered 1 to 11 and all the cards bore different pictures except numbers 11 (which were of Dan), 10 (Guest and Peabody) and 9 (Digby). This made the cards similar to a normal pack of cards and thus allowed a variation of gin rummy to be played with them. The actual rules were slightly different and someone has suggested that they were transported back in time from the future, but if the players got bored they could always try matching the pictures to those from the comic. Again, it was not original *Eagle* artwork.

Cards were not the only game to get the 'by permission of *Eagle*' on their box. As is often the case with this sort of spin-off, they were all variations on existing games, or merely current favourites with pictures of Dan stuck on. Chad Valley produced a couple of handsome bagatelles. One featured a nice piece of art, with *Anastasia* flying over Space Fleet HQ; there were points for landing on the planets in the background, while if you missed everything you were 'out of commission'. The other had the Performing Flea from 'Prisoners in Space' as the backdrop to a huddle of the main characters.

Dan Dare's Space Race was a straightforward snakes-and-ladders variation, while Rocket Ball involved a compartmentalised box into which you tried to shoot your aforementioned ball for points. Jupiter and Uranus scored ten points each, while Mars only got you one, even though it was no less difficult to hit the spot. Big Game Hunt on Venus was based on the fairground game of shooting down cardboard cut-outs and featured some of the creatures from the first adventure.

Crescent Toys produced a nice set of die-cast metal figures of some of the characters from the strip. These included Dan and Digby, of course, plus Peabody, Sondar and a final one who was probably meant to be Guest but was pretty indistinguishable from Digby other than being a millimetre taller. The final pieces were a rocket and launcher. This wasn't big enough to carry any of the figures, but was exactly the right size to take your eye out if you got too close.

When the day was done and bedtime came, the final thing to do was a little spot of reading. If you'd already read that week's comic seventeen times it was useful to have other material available, and of course the *Eagle* was happy to provide it. The literary spin-offs were many and wide-ranging. We've already seen the Presso book, which included a story as well as Wallis Rigby's cardboard *Anastasia*, and a second version was produced with a generic spaceship. Possibly more beautiful was the *Dan Dare Pop-Up Book*, published by Juvenile. There were five pages that popped up. The first shows the rockets being launched to destroy the asteroid in 'The Red Moon Mystery'. The second shows all the team working inside a roto-cruiser. Third up is a beautiful version of the Mars satellite station *SFJ2*, again from 'The Red Moon Mystery'. The penultimate scene shows the team boarding one of the Telezero reflector ships in the Venus story, before it is back to the 'Red Moon' in the final pop-up, which depicts *Anastasia* landing on the asteroid. In between, the reader gets introduced to the crew, various other characters from the first two tales, and some great drawings of a selection of space transports.

Eagle produced annuals on an, erm, annual basis, and these all had Dan Dare strips in them. Often these were quickly produced and were independent from what was happening in the strip. On many occasions the writer and artist would take the opportunity to go back in time to an earlier part of Dan's career, but not always. For completists these stories could often throw up anomalies in the 'Dan Dare' timeline. As for other Dan Dare books, the first was his *Space Book*, which appeared in 1953 and was published by Hulton itself. It included strips, and articles by eminent science writers, including one by Arthur C. Clarke, but most people head to it for Frank Hampson's opening remarks, where he discusses how he saw the early days of rocketry while serving during the war. A decade later a *Space Annual* was produced with some strips – 'The Planulid' and 'The Planet of the Shadows' – and space features such as 'Exploring the Planets', 'An American in Orbit' and 'Satellites at Work'.

The strips to be found in this and the various *Eagle* annuals are a slight anomaly and often fall outside the main canon of work. In most cases they were still overseen, but never drawn, by Frank Hampson, and there was little attempt to make them fit in with the timeline being created in the weekly stories. Thus they may be from a time before the adventures began in *Eagle* Issue 1. 'The Planulid' is set in Australia at an unidentified date. Another story, 'Mars 1988', is set in that year, drawn by Greta and Harold, and has a much younger Dan Dare being selected by Guest for what appears to be one of his first big assignments. In general these other strips were less well drawn than in the comic, and had a story that was completed in just a few pages so that they would fit nicely into an annual. They leave collectors and chroniclers the task of trying to fit everything into a logical order, which is not always possible.

There were also some 'Dan Dare' text stories in the 1963 *Space Annual*, one very presciently about a fuel shortage on Earth, and also various features on the man himself. These were mainly in the form of data sheets, with information about his vehicles, spaceships and so on. Inside the back cover was a handy guide to the various Space Fleet uniforms.

Many '*Eagle* novels' were produced. These were

purely text-based stories, as the name suggests. 'Jack O'Lantern', 'Storm Nelson' and 'Luck of the Legion' all got novelised, and so did Dan himself, in *Dan Dare on Mars* written by Basil Dawson. This was Dawson's only book, and is the only original novel written about Dare. Dawson went on to make a career in screenwriting for television. In the 1950s he wrote for the Richard Greene incarnation of Robin Hood, in the 1960s he was scripting *Emergency Ward 10*, and in the 1970s he finished off with *Crossroads* before becoming a script editor.

And finally, for those who know that philately will get you anything, there was the Dan Dare Interplanetary Stamp Folder, which was produced for Lifebuoy Soap and contained thirty-two stamps featuring Dan and friends, plus transportation, monsters and some scenes from the stories. The currency on the stamps is the 'nova', and each stamp had a short descriptive text beneath it in the album. It's an interesting crossover item that has raised eyebrows in the stamp-collecting world, as sheets keep turning up in job lots of real stamps that people buy.

At the time of writing, there is a new range of retro toys being produced. A company called Ecotronic in Bridgwater have just released a range of Dan Dare toys based on some of the classics. They are offering the Planet Gun Set, a circular jigsaw featuring art from 'Reign of the Robots', the card game and the walkie-talkie set. Whether this is a good chance for parents to rebuy their lost youth, or just to give things to their kids, it proves that, even sixty years after it all began, companies can cash in on the Dan Dare cachet.

CHAPTER EIGHT

Hampson and Morris after 'Dare'

TOGETHER Frank Hampson and Marcus Morris brought Dan Dare to the world, but when it all fell apart they left separately, and to very different futures. Marcus was forced out of *Eagle* by the strictures of the new owners and the limitations he felt that they put on him doing his job. Frank left because he felt he no longer owned or controlled the strip he had created. These two men from quite different backgrounds, having lost control of their worlds, had to walk away from the magazine they had created and which, in effect, had created them.

Actually the first thing they both did after leaving – the editor's chair in Marcus's case, and 'Dan Dare' in Frank's – was to work together for the *Eagle* – well almost together. 'The Road of Courage' was Frank's *Eagle* swansong, in which he chronicled the life of Jesus. If you were to look at the pages of the comic you would believe that Marcus wrote the scripts and Frank drew the pictures. In fact, as mentioned above, it has now come to light that Marcus had very little involvement in the scripting and merely agreed to put his name to the strip as part of his severance from the magazine, and a Reverend Guy David provided the words to Frank's artwork.

Without doubt Frank was distraught at what had happened at the end of his time with 'Dan Dare', but 'The Road of Courage' gave him all the control and freedom he could have wished for, with a trip to the Middle East thrown in for research and a little of the battery-recharging he had so desired. He didn't realise it then, but this was indeed his last work for the *Eagle*; and while this whole period was not a happy one for him, he could at least look back on a strip that secured his name among the greats, if any such security were needed. The plan when 'The Road' had first been discussed was that Frank would return to 'Dan Dare' after a year or so. (This perhaps explains why Frank Bellamy only signed up for one year.) As discussed earlier, that return never happened and thus by the end of 1961 both Marcus and Frank were no more to be seen in the corridors of the *Eagle* offices.

When the *Eagle* door slammed shut behind Marcus, another one opened in front of him, and what a door it was. It took him into the office of the editorial director of the National Magazine Company, and just three years later, in 1964, he became managing director. The major achievements during his time at the company now known simply as NatMags were to merge *Queen* and *Harper's Bazaar* into *Harper's & Queen*, and the launch of the UK version of *Cosmopolitan* and later of *Company*. His career at NatMags took him all the way through to retirement in 1984, and his success in publishing is marked by an award given in his name. Since 1990 the Periodical Publishers Association has given an annual Marcus Morris Award to someone who has made a significant and long-standing contribution to the magazine-publishing business. Marcus received an OBE in 1983 for his services to publishing.

If life after the *Eagle* went well for Marcus, it was not such plain sailing for Frank. For those who believe in such things, it appears that a lot of Frank's problems came from within. He just couldn't get over the fact that someone else owned 'Dan Dare', and this badly affected his health and self-confidence. His reputation also took something of a battering, as Bruce Cornwell recalls: 'I heard all the rumours and gossip and "Frank Hampson" was a dirty word. They wouldn't touch him with a bargepole. He was too expensive. He was not reliable on his time. And of course as far as editing goes in publishing you've got to be on date, on time, when you commit yourself. Unfortunately he blotted his copybook properly.'

It is worth remembering that Frank and Bruce were not always bosom buddies, but the truth of what Bruce says lies in the fact that the artist who had created the best-selling comic of the 1950s could not get regular work, certainly not with any of the weekly publications. He did get the odd commission, such as a couple of drawings for a Bovril advertising campaign, which quite poignantly became the last Hampson drawings to appear in the *Eagle*.

Bruce felt that it was a waste of a great talent that Frank couldn't, or rather wouldn't, bend to the realities of the publishing world. 'He was almost chopped off. No one would touch him. But it was still the same sort of work, same sort of problems. If he did anything else it would have been the same problems throughout and it was a rotten shame I think. The industry couldn't cope with it. It's just a rotten shame.'

Frank did eventually find a home for his talent, thanks to Douglas Keen, the man behind Ladybird Books, who was a big fan of his work. From 1964 he worked sporadically for them on classic books such as the Nursery Rhymes, Kings and Queens and Food Through the Ages series.

In April 1969 the *Eagle* disappeared from the newsagents' shelves, and the next year its creator had another crisis when he was diagnosed with throat cancer. As an almost lifelong pipe smoker the cause seems quite obvious, but he would probably have admitted that his ongoing anger and bitterness at his treatment over 'Dan Dare' did not help his health. He even referred to a 'canker' in his memories of Dare in his interview with Alan Vince. Fortunately though the disease responded to treatment and by the end of 1973 the future looked favourable, healthwise at least.

Frank took his years of experience into teaching, with work at Ewell Technical College and Epsom College of Art, but in 1975 he finally found the world-wide recognition that his work has deserved. The International Exhibition of Comics, which was held bi-annually in the Italian city of Lucca between 1968 and 1992, was run by Rinaldo Traini, a publisher of comics and writer of books on the subject.

A jury of fellow comic-strip artists declared Frank the best writer and illustrator of comics since the Second World War, gave him the title 'Prestigioso Maestro' and presented him with a small statue of the Yellow Kid, who had been the lead character in 'Hogan's Alley', a strip set in New York and drawn by Richard F. Outcault. This recognition from his peers meant everything to Frank, and although it could never make up for the loss he felt it did at least bring some comfort to him in his final years and sparked renewed public interest in him and his work.

Throughout the 1970s there were reprints of some of the best work from the strip, and every time one of these books came out there was the hope that Frank would be involved and that it might even lead to a relaunch of the strip with him in charge. There was even talk of a television series. But in the end all of these came to nought and in a way it must have been like a slow death. The small chinks of hope in the gloom, the merest possibility of getting something back from the work he had put in all those years before, always ending up with nothing.

Peter remembers his father being reluctant to discuss his time on the *Eagle* with anyone.

He didn't enjoy talking about it. The whole time when it blew and broke up and he left the *Eagle* was not a particularly happy time and he fell out with Marcus and so it wasn't really talked about. He didn't really talk to anyone about it, he was iffy about answering fan mail, although I think he did. It really only came back up again with the Lucca thing, the Yellow Kid.

I remember some comic conventions around that time, and framing stuff up for him to hang on the walls. But I don't remember much about Lucca other than he came back with the Yellow Kid. Mum was really chuffed to have it, although any sort of memory with Dan Dare always had a dark side to it because of the circumstances that led up to the ending of it.

The only thing he did full-time was Ewell Tech. He worked there for four or five years as a graphics technician and he enjoyed that. That was the only time really that he wasn't self-employed.

Dorothy was always vital to Frank's work, both in terms of her moral support and as a steadying influence:

She married a struggling artist, actually not even a struggling artist; she married someone who was in the army, back end of the war. And sort of then this rollercoaster that was 'Dan Dare' started in 1950 and she was swept along with it.

She just sort of kept him going. She was very supportive all the time. She didn't have any input in an artistic sense towards the artistic output but she was an absolute rock as far as he was concerned. She was always there, there all day, making coffee, just giving support. He probably couldn't have done it without her. She was absolutely rock-solid all the way through, and in later years when he was ill as well. She was just always, always there. She did it without making a fuss about it.

She was a very, very even-tempered, very quiet, very kind, very supportive person. She just went along with it.

Frank described his post-*Eagle* years in just a few matter-of-fact sentences for the 1978 interview:

> I worked for Ladybird books till I got cancer and then when I got cancer of the throat I stopped working for Labybird, drew out my life insurance and went to Samarkand where I'd always wanted to go before I died . . . And then I didn't die . . . which was awkward for everybody concerned so I got this job at North East Surrey College of Technology. At Ladybird, I did nine [books] altogether, I forget all the titles. *The Times* were very nice about them last week.

As the interview is drawing to a close he explains how he has been studying for the Open University, and that he is now in his third year. 'I was enjoying it so much I thought I'd have a go at doubling up and doing two [modules] just to get the degree a bit faster . . . Well I mean, I want "BA" on the headstone. [He folds his hands, his long elegant fingers, and looks at the camera.] I want to be buried with dignity.' As the interviewer explains that she has asked all her questions unless he has anything left to add, Frank continues looking at the camera, almost as though he is about to speak again but is searching for what to say. He just looks into the lens with his hands in his lap as the cameraman says something inaudible, and the picture fades to black.

Frank died on 8 July 1985. Just under four years later, on 16 March 1989, Marcus Morris followed.

As the person who is now the touchstone for his father's work, Peter Hampson carries the best wishes of Frank's army of fans.

I'm just happy to be able to tell them as much as I can. I understand where they are coming from. I know the sort of things which may fire them up. Every now and then I come up with something. At the fiftieth do in Southport I took some pieces up and when we were there they asked me to give a talk. One of the things I took was the Yellow Kid, which is in a [presentation] box. Halfway through the talk I said I had the Yellow Kid and flipped it open and there was an audible gasp. I suppose it was something to see in the flesh. It's nice to be able to do that sort of thing.

CHAPTER NINE

The Future:
Infinity and beyond?

NASA DOES NOT HAVE a mandatory retirement age for astronauts, but generally pilots hang up their helmets at sixty. In 2010 Dan Dare reached that very age, but is showing no signs of leaving the hangar for the last time.

Apart from his fan-fuelled exploits in *Spaceship Away*, it seemed for a while Dan may have taken a back seat in the comic-strip world, until Richard Branson's Virgin Comics produced a seven-part series created by two major players in the strip world. It was written by Garth Ennis and drawn by Gary Erskine, who had previously worked together on *Judge Dredd*.

Branson has long been known as one of Dare's biggest fans, so his attempt to get him back into action is no surprise. The story is set ten years after Frank Hampson's era, and starts with Dan enjoying a quiet retirement. Before long, though, he is the only man who can save the planet. (All issues of the comic are now sold out, but are collected together in a Dynamite Entertainment compendium.)

At the moment there are no plans for a further comic series, but as ever there are talks of a film. In a world of PlayStations, hand-held computers on which you can watch live television, and children with the average attention span of a gnat, is it possible that a hero created in the 1950s can find a new audience among the browsers of the Blu-ray shelves? The answer is probably yes, because the fact of the matter is that the highest-grossing films of the last ten years all involve a superhero of one sort or another. From the rebooted Batman series to the *Pirates of the Caribbean* franchise and even Harry Potter, film fans love a hero. (The last of these three proves that modernity is not vital, being set in an England as different from what we know as Frank's fictional country ever was.)

Whenever a Dan Dare film is mentioned, two things come to mind. The first is that it was talk of a film that seemed to be the straw that broke Frank Hampson's back and led to him leaving the strip. The second is, of course, who could possibly play Dan?

At the 2010 Comic-Con in San Diego it was formally announced that Warner Brothers have acquired the rights to Dan Dare. There is no information yet on the plot of the film, the possible director or any other details, but when this film finally hits the screen it will be a world-wide event.

More likely to appear on screens before that is a television drama about the lives of Frank Hampson and Marcus Morris and the magazine they created. The story of the creation and evolution of the *Eagle* and the changing relationship of its two founders would make for a fascinating and intelligent drama with as many twists and turns as any Dan Dare plot.

What is clear is that Dan Dare is as much a part of British culture as he ever was. Proof of this came in April 2008 when the Science Museum in London opened an exhibition entitled Dan Dare & the Birth of Hi-Tech Britain. There are many public figures both real and fictional who could have been chosen to head up this special display, but Dan was chosen above all. This is because of the inventiveness of the strip itself, the creation of both fantastic spaceships and everyday technology summing up the pioneer spirit of Britain in the 1950s and 1960s that the museum was showcasing. Originally planned to run for six months, the exhibition was extended again and again, and at the time of writing is set to run until March 2011. Maybe this is to coincide with the fictional date that Dan returned to find the planet under the reign of the Mekon's robots, although it is more than likely it will be extended again. The amazing thing is that it is not just seventy-year-old men who have been seen poring over the artefacts, photos and displays. It is something that has stirred the imagination of all ages, just as the strip did when it first appeared. Since the exhibition opened over five million people have been through the doors of the Science Museum.

And so, as Dan enters his seventh decade, he has clearly fulfilled Frank Hampson's name for him; he remains the Pilot of the Future.

The Science Museum in London has used Dan as a main draw for its exhibition, Dan Dare and the Birth of Hi-Tech Britain.

Stamps from Dan's universe.

Eagle Club

Rules

1. *Members of the EAGLE CLUB will*
   - (a) Enjoy life and help others to enjoy life. They will not enjoy themselves at the expense of others.
   - (b) Make the best of themselves. They will develop themselves in body, in mind, and in spirit. They will tackle things for themselves and not wait for others to do things for them.
   - (c) Work with others for the good of all around them.
   - (d) Always lend a hand to those in need of help. They will not shirk difficult or dangerous jobs.

2. *The EAGLE CLUB exists*
   - (a) For comradeship between all who accept the rules given above.
   - (b) To honour acts of courage and high achievement of any kind by awarding special certificates and badges.
   - (c) To organise meetings and expeditions for members.

I D Grantham accept the aims of the EAGLE CLUB as here set forth, and promise to keep the rules.

Signed: D Grantham

Date 20-2-1951

Name David Grantham

Address The Argosy Millstrood Rd Whitstable KENT

Age 10 years

School Whitstable boys

Local club (if any)

If found please return this card to the H.O. of the EAGLE CLUB, 43 Shoe Lane, London, EC4.

The accoutrements of being a member of The Eagle Club were worth the joining fee alone.

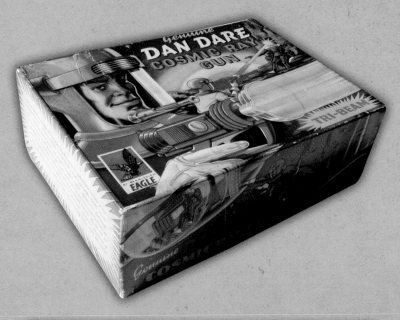

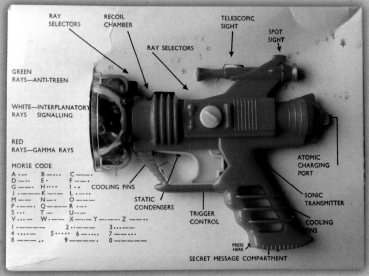

When on another planet you need to make sure you have your instructions to hand.

When broadcasting it is important
to have state of the art equipment

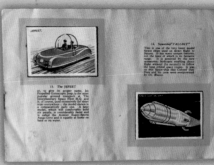

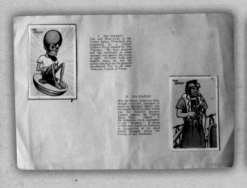

Signed by Frank Hampson, pages from
the Calvert Tooth Powder Album.

Card games, board games and film; it didn't matter if it was raining outside.

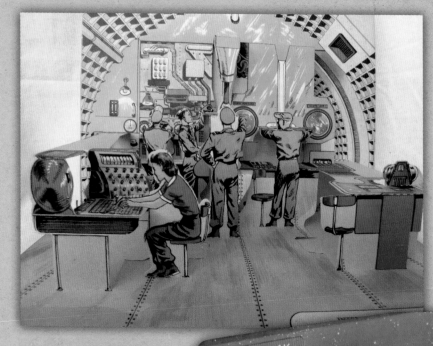

The Dan Dare Presso pop-up book. A masterpiece.

APPENDIX

The Dan Dare Adventures

✳ 'Dan Dare – Pilot of the Future'
(often referred to now as 'Voyage to Venus')

14 April 1950 (no. 1) to 28 September 1951 (Vol. 2, no. 25)

Date set: July 1995 to 21 July 1996
Main characters: Dan, Digby, Sir Hubert, Hank, Pierre, Peabody, Sondar, Voltan
Villain: the Mekon
Location: Earth and Venus

The food on Earth is running out and Dan and the crew offer the last chance of reaching Venus and a hopefully bounteous food source. All six manage to land on the planet and discover it is inhabited by three distinct species: the Treens, the Therons and the Atlantines.

The Treens, ruled by the Mekon, are only interested in research and furthering their knowledge of the universe. The Mekon rules the northern hemisphere of Venus from his capital city Mekonta. The Therons are a peace-loving, highly developed people who have created a world where no one needs to work as machines do it all for them. The Atlantines are a slave race for the Treens and are descended from humans whom the Treens abducted many years previously.

The Mekon is eager to use Earth for experiments and the furtherance of science, and plans to destroy anything and anyone that gets in his way. With the help of the Therons and Atlantines, Dan and co. manage to overcome his evil plans and set up a relay system for bringing food back home. Special mention also goes to Digby's Aunt Anastasia.

✳

✳ 'The Red Moon Mystery'

5 October 1951 (Vol. 2, no. 26) to 20 June 1952 (Vol. 3, no. 11)

Date set: September 1999 to 30 October 1999
Main characters: Dan, Digby, Sir Hubert, Hank, Pierre, Peabody, Sondar,
   Ivor Dare
Villain: Space Bees
Location: Earth and Mars

While holidaying on Mars, Dan takes Digby to visit his Uncle Ivor, who is making an archaeological study of the planet. A call comes in from Sir Hubert to go and investigate an asteroid, the 'red moon', which is on a collision course with Earth.

The Red Moon, Ivor discovers, was the cause of the annihilation of the Martian race. Using magnetic forces, the Space Bees on the asteroid manoeuvre it through space in search of food, indicated by the light emitted from planets, which gives them a chlorophyll signature. By creating a ghost signal the team manage to lure the Red Moon away from Earth, thus saving everyone. When it is far enough away, they blow it up. But are they killed in the blast?

✳ 'Marooned on Mercury'

27 June 1952 (Vol. 3, no. 12) to 20 February 1953 (Vol. 3, no. 46)

Date set: 30 October 1999 to the end of 1999
Main characters: Dan, Digby, Peabody, Sondar, Urb, Willie, Samson
Villain: the Mekon
Location: Mercury

The blast from the Red Moon has thrown Sondar's ship into outer space with no control or power. Eventually it is dragged into the atmosphere of Mercury and crashes on the surface.

The crew are saved from the harsh environment of the planet by some Mercurians, although at first they are not sure if they are friendly. Unknown to Dan, the Mekon is also on Mercury and is using Fay-Saw, grown on Mercury, to make a deadly compound called Panthanaton which he plans to use to destroy life on Venus and then Earth. He plans to use Dan and other Space Fleet pilots to fly the ships that will carry this deadly cargo.

The Mekon has enslaved the Mercurians to harvest Fay-Saw, but Dan manages to rouse the populace against him. The Mekon escapes to fight another day, while Dan destroys all the stock of Panthanaton and returns, triumphant, to Earth.

✳ 'Operation Saturn'

27 February 1953 (Vol. 3, no. 47) to 21 May 1954 (Vol. 5, no. 21)

Date set: sometime in 2000
Main characters: Dan, Digby, Peabody, Sir Hubert, Hank, Pierre, Sondar
Villains: Dr Blasco and Vora
Location: Earth and Saturn

Space Fleet ships have been subjected to attacks from 'Black Cats', which bore holes in them, resulting in death for all aboard. After investigating the latest attack it is discovered by Dr Blasco that they have come from Saturn.

Saturn is so far away it is thought impossible to reach until Dan, through numerous test flights, finds a way to stabilise the superfuel monatomic hydrogen. By coincidence it is Blasco who has invented the equipment to do this.

The crew, along with Blasco and his team of scientists, set off for Saturn. On the way Blasco reveals himself as a villain, intent on taking over Earth with the help of his allies, the High Lords of Saturn. He imprisons Dan and co. and plans to hold them till they reach their destination, where they will be used as entertainment for the cruel games of their hosts. Dan and Digby escape to one of Saturn's moons, Phoebe, and join forces (eventually) with the Pirates of Tharl.

With this help they save the rest of the crew, but are captured and sent to meet their fate at the hands of Vora, ruler of Saturnia. Vora wants Dan to tell him about Tharl's planned revolt, but Dan refuses in spite of inhuman torture. The 'Black Cats', Kroopaks, are sent to destroy Earth, but Sondar manages to send a signal for them to self-destruct. Defeated and powerless without his Kroopaks, Vora commits suicide, and Earth is saved.

✳

✳ 'Prisoners of Space'

28 May 1954 (Vol. 5, no. 22) to 6 May 1955 (Vol. 6, no. 18)

Date set: 2001
Main characters: Dan, Digby, Peabody, Sir Hubert, Hank, Pierre, Sondar,
   Steve Valiant, Flamer Spry, Groupie
Villain: the Mekon
Location: Earth, Venus and Space

While being shown around the top-secret new spaceship the *Performing Flea*, Astral College cadets Flamer Spry and Steve Valiant accidentally hit the launch button and along with their guide, Groupie, are sent on a pre-set course to Space Station XQY.

On arrival they discover the CO dead and the space station under the control of the Mekon. The cadets and Groupie are quickly captured, and the Mekon offers to exchange them for Dare. He is to come alone and unarmed. Dan knows it could mean death, but he has to save the others. Unknown to him, Digby hides in the ship to offer help.

On arrival Dan is double-crossed by the Mekon, who plans to kill them all. Thanks to the stowed-away Digby, Dan escapes and sends a message to Earth that the space station should be destroyed on his signal; at last the Mekon will be finished. Not all goes to plan, and Dan is thought dead when the *Flea* is blown up. The Mekon decides to send Groupie and Valiant into orbit around the Earth in a space bubble, as punishment for defying him.

An Elite Squadron arrives from Earth to destroy the space station but the Mekon manages to escape just in time and heads for Venus. Believing Dare dead, he thinks he can now reassert his supremacy.

Dare, Valiant and Groupie get to Venus but are quickly captured and sentenced to death, ironically via the bombs of their own ships, which are heading to Venus to attack the Mekon. As the missiles are about to strike Guest realises it is Dan and calls them off. Dan and co. escape, and the Mekon has to run again – but Dan convinces him that his ship has a limpet mine attached. As Dare 'never lies', the Mekon abandons ship and puts himself into the space bubble he had aimed to use for Valiant and Groupie. Dare captures the Mekon and sends him off to a rehabilitation centre on Venus. The Mekon's final words are 'They will live to rue the day they spared my life!'

* 'The Man from Nowhere'

13 May 1955 (Vol. 6, no. 19) to 25 November 1955 (Vol. 6, no. 47)

Date set: end of 2001 to mid-2002
Main characters: Dan, Digby, Flamer Spry, Lex O'Malley, Lero
Villains: the Phants
Location: Earth, Cryptos

This story opens with one of Frank Hampson's most famous pieces of work: the Venusian Embassy party. The party is to celebrate the return of peace in the universe and shows practically the whole cast list of 'Dan Dare' characters. The story is also of note as it introduces a new character who would become a stalwart over the next few years: Commander Lex O'Malley.

The party is interrupted due to an alert at Space Fleet when a spaceship of no known design suddenly appears, as if from nowhere, on the screens. Dan, Digby and O'Malley board one of three interceptor craft to go and investigate. As they approach the strange ship, it does not respond to radio calls and Dan is about to open fire when there is an explosion on the ship. Only Digby sees that a cigar-shaped craft has shot clear of the blast. The ship carries on its trajectory towards Earth.

Dan reports to Space Fleet HQ that he believes it must have been travelling at the speed of light to appear as suddenly as it did. The wreckage is sought and eventually found. The crew are still alive and Lero, the commander, delivers his message. He and his crew have travelled across the universe to seek Dan's help. They come from Cryptos and need Dan to return with them to fight against the Phants, a cruel race who, every 10,000 years, attack and destroy everyone on Cryptos. It is decided that Dan, Digby, Lex and Flamer will go with Lero to help in the fight.

The destination is very far but can be made in a short space of time, apparently, by the Crypts' ability to travel at the speed of light. On arrival it appears that they are too late: the attack has already begun. Dan and co. spring into action and manage to bring down a Phant fighter, the first such destruction in the history of the conflict between the two planets, but then Dan's ship is hit. Just before it is totally destroyed all the crew manage to evacuate in their individual space torpedoes. But can they survive? The story closes with the torpedoes hurtling towards the planet Cryptos and Flamer not responding to Dan's desperate calls.

* 'Rogue Planet'

2 December 1955 (Vol. 6, no. 48) to 15 February 1957 (Vol. 8, no. 7)

Date set: March 2007 to 2011
Main characters: Dan, Digby, Flamer Spry, Lex O'Malley, Lero, Stripey
Villains: the Phants
Location: Earth, Cryptos

This story continues on from 'The Man from Nowhere'. The torpedoes land on a geyser island on Cryptos, but Flamer is nowhere to be found. Leaving the Kruxes behind to look for him, the rest escape off the island to reach the main settlements. En route they hear the Great War Drum, which signals that the invasion has begun. Their numbers are increased when they are befriended by a black-and-white-striped miniature elephant-type creature, whom they name Stripey.

They continue on their way and come across a troupe of Phants. They manage to overcome them and strand them on a geyser island.

Having not eaten for days, Lex finds some food on the Phant vehicle they have taken, in the form of capsules. He downs one and within a couple of minutes becomes a wild thing intent on destruction. The crew restrain him and Lero shows them the Crypts' rations of yellow pills, which contrast to the purple Phant ration. Dan starts to wonder if this difference is linked to the warlike nature of the Phants and the passive nature of the Crypts.

Before the slaughter due under the 10,000-year cycle, a whole generation of Crypts and indigenous animals are sent away in the *Kra*, an Ark-like ship, so that their descendants can return in many years' time to repopulate the planet in readiness for the next Phant invasion.

Lex takes over a Phant food-capsule factory and switches the output so that the warlike race begin to eat the peace-making food. And thus peace is brought to the land. The *Kra* is recalled and Dan, Lex, Digby, Flamer and Stripey are lionised as the people who brought peace between the Crypts and the Phants.

Lero gives them his ship to go back home, but hands Dan a letter with some shocking news. Dan waits until they are on board before he spills the beans. Those beans are that the trip to Cryptos took five years, not a few weeks. They did not travel at the speed of light but were put into suspended animation by Lero and the trip home will take the same time. While they will not age, everyone they know back on Earth will be ten years older than when they last saw them.

✳ 'Reign of the Robots'

22 February 1957 (Vol. 8, no. 8) to 24 January 1958 (Vol. 9, no. 4)

Date set: 2011
Main characters: Dan, Digby, Flamer Spry, Lex O'Malley, Stripey
Villain: the Mekon
Location: Earth, Venus

This story continues straight on from 'Rogue Planet'. The crew return from Cryptos to find Earth deserted. An eerie silence hangs over the planet. They discover that the Sanctum, a top-secret hide-out for the world's leaders, has been taken over by the Mekon. He has been awaiting their return for nine years. Under his command he now has battalions of Elektrobots and Selektrobots.

The Mekon is using the Earth's population to recreate all the great discoveries of mankind. Dan and co. are captured, given a tour of the ghastly laboratory that the Earth now is, and then put to work with the rest of its inhabitants. Sir Hubert, Peabody, Hank and Pierre have all been kept in suspended animation as hostages for Dan's return in the creepy House of Silence.

They soon find pockets of resistance as they meet up with Space Fleet men and former cadets, who are now all ten years older. Flamer comes up with a cunning plan to impersonate the Mekon and get the robots to destroy each other.

Digby pretends to surrender to the Mekon and is taken on as an overseer of the experiments. They are all taken to Venus, but on the journey Dan escapes and discovers a Sargasso Sea of Space, into which every Space Fleet ship that has ever disappeared has been drawn. He also finds two old Space Fleet pilots, King and Macfarlane, who have been marooned with no means of escape. They find *Anastasia* and make contact with the Mekon, who threatens Dan's friends with death if he refuses to give himself up. Of course Dan accepts the swap.

But he sends King and Macfarlane in the Treen cruiser he escaped in, while he will travel in *Anastasia*, which the Mekon does not know exists. Now Flamer has the chance to put his own plan into action. O'Malley knocks the Mekon off his chair, Flamer sends the message to the robots and then destroys the microphone. It's a good plan and the Elektrobots begin to self-destruct almost instantly, but Flamer did not press the button that would have also sent the message to the more powerful, élite squads of Selektrobots whom the Mekon had summoned just prior to being de-chaired; so he is still the only one who can stop them and thus has the nap hand.

The only way to defeat the Selektrobots is to destroy the control satellite. It would be a suicide mission, but there is no other option, and no one else to do it but Dan.

Sir Hubert refuses to let Dan die. Taking *Anastasia*, he follows the warhead piloted by Dan. Dan sets the warhead to strike and bails out in a space bubble though he knows he won't survive the blast. The warhead wreaks its damage; Dan is blasted out of his space bubble into space; Sir Hubert picks him up, but he is not breathing by the time they are back on *Anastasia*. It appears once more that Dan has met his maker.

* ### 'The Ship That Lived'

31 January 1958 (Vol. 9, no. 5) to 18 April 1958 (Vol. 9, no. 16)

Date set: 2011
Main characters: Dan, Digby, Flamer Spry, Lex O'Malley, Stripey
Villain: the Mekon
Location: Earth, Venus

This story picks up from the end of 'Reign of the Robots'. With Dan unconscious, Sir Hubert is piloting *Anastasia* as Treen attack ships approach. O'Malley tries to persuade the Mekon to call off the attack in return for his life, but the Mekon knows that O'Malley will not kill a prisoner. Digby, Flamer, Mac and King take up two Treen ships to defend *Anastasia* but they arrive too late and she hurtles, on fire and out of control, towards the Flamebelt.

Sir Hubert is trapped away from the controls but manages to rouse Dan, who takes the stick and pulls the ship up, managing a landing on the belt. The fire is out, but now the silicon mass moves in for the kill on the stricken ship, Dan and Guest. Pierre and Hank arrive with two hover-chairs, but Pierre loses control of one and now all four of them seem doomed.

Dan comes up with a plan to use hydrogen-inflated space suits, which enables them to escape, but *Annie* is still sinking. Just then Volstar arrives with fluorine grenades, which are used to keep the silicon mass at bay while *Anastasia* is hoisted clear.

During the celebrations at saving the ship, the Mekon escapes. He sends a message to 'the Last Three' about Plan X.X., and hurls himself into an object that emerges from the boiling-hot sands. It sinks and he's gone.

✳ 'Phantom Fleet'

25 April 1958 (Vol. 9, no. 17) to 27 December 1958 (Vol. 9, no. 52)

Date set: from this point on the dates when the stories are set are not clear
Main characters: Dan, Digby, Peabody, Hank, Pierre, Stripey, the Cosmobes
Villains: the Pescods
Location: Moon, Earth

On a routine flight back from the moon, Dan and Digby's ship suffers a loss of communication. It soon becomes clear that electronic communication is out all over the Space Fleet network.

They manage to get back to Earth in *Anastasia*, and find that the cause of the interference is a group of ships from the far-off planet I-Cos. The Cosmobes have been travelling space to discover a new home after the water on their planet dried up. Time is against them, and Earth is their last resort, as they are being pursued by their enemy from home, the Pescods.

Dan persuades the Earth Government to allow some of the Cosmobes to land in return for their help in fighting off the Pescods, whose fleet has just got to Venus and seems able to destroy anything in its path. Everything seems hopeless as the Pescods' weapon, the Crimson Death, is all-powerful. Peabody, with the help of the Cosmobes, discovers that a rubber compound offers protection against it, but still there seems no way to fight them off.

The Pescods land on Earth and begin to drill into the volcanic rock at the bottom of the ocean, to create a base to hide their ships. Unknown to them, though, this will be their downfall. The place they have chosen is the heart of Krakatao, an underwater volcano. They bore deeper and deeper until finally Krakatao explodes and blows them to kingdom come.

The Cosmobes are given permission to live on Earth as thanks for their help.

✳ 'Safari in Space'

3 January 1959 (Vol. 10, no. 1) to 2 May 1959 (Vol. 10, no. 18)

Main characters: Dan, Digby, Flamer, Peabody, Sir Hubert, O'Malley
Villain: Galileo McHoo
Location: Venus, McHoo asteroid

Dan, Digby and Flamer have gone to Venus for a safari on the uninhabited island of Maraku. Therex is their Theronian host. While Digby stays at camp to cook, the others go off to the Black Lake.

As they climb down to the water Flamer throws a stone into the murky depths and awakens the beast below. Dan and Therex have to act quickly to save the boy. Back at the camp they discover that Digby and *Anastasia* have gone.

As everyone begins to search for Dig, Dan and Flamer are taken too and winched up into an Earth ship. They're tied up and left to wait by the crew, whose uniforms bear the insignia AD TERRA NOVA.

Also holidaying on Venus are Sir Hubert, Professor Peabody and O'Malley. They too are picked up and join Dan and Flamer in the hold of the *Caledonian*. They are taken to the McHoo asteroid and brought before their captor, Galileo McHoo.

McHoo explains how his Uncle Copernicus founded the first interplanetary freight service, the Cosmic Line, and the Cosmic building yards. The money the clan made was used for further research into space. His father, Halley, discovered a planet similar to Earth in the outer reaches of the universe, which he named Terra Nova. He designed and built a ship to get there. The ship was piloted by Copernicus and . . . Dan's father.

Dan remembers his father being the chief test pilot for Cosmic Space Ships but believed that he was lost on a test flight in the *Scotia*. McHoo explains that he was indeed lost on a test flight, but it was on the *Galactic Pioneer*. Halley was killed in the blast from the take-off, the asteroid base was destroyed and Galileo has spent his life rebuilding it. One message from the ship was found among the wreckage of the base. It read 'Take-off Complete. Safe on Course. Accelerating to Schedule.' A note and a ring were left for Dan by his father at the Cosmic yards.

McHoo is convinced that the flight was a success and that Dan's father lived. He has rebuilt the base and a ship, the *Galactic Galleon*, with the aim of reaching Terra Nova, and he has kidnapped Dan and the crew to make that voyage. They have no choice but to agree. Dan, anyway, is eager to go and the rest will always follow him.

As McHoo shows them the ship, Space Fleet cruisers appear on the radars. They have been informed of the kidnapping, and the *Caledonian*'s flight will have been picked up on Space Fleet radars. McHoo will not be defeated, and brings forward the launch. Dan confesses to Sir Hubert that he wants McHoo to get away with it: he wants to know what happened to his father.

The ship, with its Halley Drive, speeds away from the chasing Space Fleet cruisers and off to Terra Nova.

✳ 'Terra Nova'

9 May 1959 (Vol. 10, no. 19) to 21 November 1959 (Vol. 10, no. 40)

Main characters: Dan, Digby, Flamer, Peabody, Sir Hubert, O'Malley
Villains: the Nagrab
Location: Space, Terra Nova

As they hurtle through space, the *Galactic Galleon* seems to be hit by meteors. Dan, Digby, Sir Hubert, Flamer and Lex investigate and decide the damage was made by bullets. At that moment, the ship disappears from beneath them as the engines are cut, but they carry on moving. Peabody has to take control of the *Galactic Galleon* to try to find her friends, which she eventually does.

Soon afterwards they arrive at Terra Nova and there, in orbit, is the floating ship from thirty years before, the *Galactic Pioneer*. Dan and Digby fly over to it in *Anastasia*. Dan boards, to find there's been an explosion. He discovers the lifeless body of Copernicus and a discharge tube with its lifeboat missing. They head back to the *Galactic Galleon* and decide to head down to the planet as Dan's father must have done so.

Once Dan, Dig and Sir Hubert land, they find the Novad city of Pax. A native speaks English and, showing them a statue of Dare Sr, explains how Dan's father helped them and then, ten years ago, left to explore the other side of the planet. It is a place far beyond where any Novad has gone. Before Dan and co. can set off to search for him, the city is attacked by the big threat to the Novads, the Nagrab, a species of giant ant.

Having had no word from the planet, Peabody, Lex and Flamer fly down and become embroiled in the battle with the Nagrab. Using *Anastasia*'s firepower they overcome the ants and Dan destroys them for ever. He now becomes a hero to the Novads, as was his father.

Rax, a Novad, describes Dare Sr's departure. He had no boat, no craft. The last they saw of him was a shining steady light in the distance across the sea. As the crew arrive back on the *Galactic Galleon* for supplies before going after Dare Sr, Dan realises what the light means.

✳ 'Trip to Trouble'

28 November 1959 (Vol. 10, no. 41) to 12 March 1960 (Vol. 11, no. 11)

Main characters: Dan, Digby, O'Malley, Calo
Villain: Grandax
Location: Terra Nova

In order to find his father, Dan plans to copy his journey. As it is overseas, Lex goes in a raft, with Dan and Digby following in *Anastasia*. Lex is caught by the Gazites and Dan meets Calo, a Lantorite, who informs him that his father was captured by the

Gazites. He gives Dan the news that the Gazites killed Dare Sr, who was helping Calo's people to fight them.

Dan asks Calo to help him free Lex from the Gazites' HQ at Lantor. They succeed but discover that Grandax, the leader of the Gazites, intends an attack on the Lantorite villages as reprisal. Dan and co. manage to thwart the attack, destroy the Gazite air fleet and capture Grandax. He manages to escape but is killed in the pursuit.

With the knowledge that his father is dead, and having finished the job that Dare Sr started, Dan returns to Earth.

＊ 'Project Nimbus'

19 March 1960 (Vol. 11, no. 12) to 9 July 1960 (Vol. 11, no. 28)

Main characters: Dan, Digby, Sir Hubert, Hank, Pierre
Villains: the Schmurds
Location: Earth, Space, Jupiter's moon

Prototype spaceship *Nimbus One* has disappeared and Dan is sent to find her. He and Digby head to Spa-1, the most sensitive radio telescope in the fleet, to see if they can spot her. The scope picks up ten blips near Jupiter, where the ship was last reported. There were ten crew members on *Nimbus One*.

Sir Hubert sends the *Andromeda* to investigate, but Dan doesn't want to miss the fun and persuades Sir Hubert to join him and the others in going out there in *Nimbus Two*. As they get near, they can hear one of the *Nimbus One* crew talking deliriously into his helmet mike. They manage to rescue them and ask what happened: the ship was boarded by 'White Creatures'. They realise that the alien ship took *Nimbus One* for its supplies.

On one of Jupiter's moons they spot a gleam of metal and investigate. It is a robotic sentry from the alien ship, which they destroy. Dig and Dan enter the mine and encounter two of the aliens. They discover that they are starving to death when Dig's food is grabbed off him, but they eat a whole vitamin block, which is too much in one go, so Dan and Digby overpower them and escape. The aliens head back to their cruiser, and the team follow.

Having found the mother ship and destroyed the space pirates, they find *Nimbus One* hidden away deep in the mine on the moon.

✳ 'Mission of the Earthmen'

16 July 1960 (Vol. 11, no. 29) to 24 December 1960 (Vol. 11, no. 52)

Main characters: Dan, Digby
Villains: the Rhogans, the Voltans
Location: Zyl, Vort

Millions of miles from Earth, Dan and Digby are scouting a new planet, Zyl, when their ship, the *Nimrod*, loses all power because of the planet's inhabitants firing at them with the Magnetron. They hurtle towards the planet's surface.

The Zylans, a highly advanced race, wish to bring civilisation to their neighbouring planet of Vort, but don't know how to. Dan and Digby set off to do it for them.

There are two peoples on the planet, Vortans and Rhogans, who are continually at war. Because of their clothes, Dan and Digby are thought by both sides to be magicians or witches. They scare everyone with their spaceship and convince them that the only way they will leave them alone is if the two sides call a truce. Common sense prevails, a truce is called and Dan and Digby leave.

In return for their help the Zylans give them a fantastic new spaceship, the *Zybalt*, to get back to the base camp that Sir Hubert has set up on one of the outer moons. But when they get there it is deserted. A message from Sir Hubert says he had to get back to Earth for a dire emergency. He doesn't explain but has left supplies for them and promises to return to pick them up. He doesn't know they now have a brilliant long-range spaceship, and so Dan and Digby set off for Earth in the *Zybalt*.

✳ 'The Solid Space Mystery'

31 December 1960 (Vol. 11, no. 53) to 10 June 1961 (Vol. 12, no. 23)

Main characters: Dan, Digby, Sir Hubert, Hank, Pierre
Villain: the Mekon
Location: Space, Earth

Hurtling back towards the solar system, the boys stop just before hitting 'solid space'. Any ship hitting it at speed is destroyed, and thus the freight lines are in chaos and the world economy is in tatters.

While shadowing a test flight of a new radar that is being piloted by Captain Long, Dan realises that the solid space is magnetic. If you hit it at speed you explode, if you go through it slowly it makes you feel drunk. His Zyl ship *Zybalt* automatically avoids the areas and protects the occupants from its effects. Earth scientists are given this vital information.

The crucial ingredient for this protection against solid space is 'indium', which is mined on Diemos, a Martian moon. Dan and Digby set off, load up with indium and head back for Earth, but encounter what they think is a Treen ship which also seems capable of speeding through the solid space. They radio Sondar, who tells them it isn't a Treen ship, so they head off in pursuit. They can't find the ship but they do find a satellite that is emitting a beam of intense energy. The strange ship appears, announces itself as Treen, and they meet the pilot, who tells them that Sondar knows nothing of their plan because they serve . . . the Mekon.

The Mekon tries unsuccessfully to kill Dan and Digby, but Pierre and Hank come to the rescue. After thrust and counterthrust they think they have the Mekon, but he sends a bacteria missile aimed at Earth to give himself the chance to get away. They destroy this, then chase him down. They destroy his ship, but unknown to them he escapes just in time.

They head back to Earth, having stopped the satellite's destabilising beam.

✳ 'The Platinum Planet'

17 June 1961 (Vol. 12, no. 24) to 25 November 1961 (Vol. 12, no. 47)

Main characters: Dan, Digby, Zeb
Villains: Astorat the Great, Lord of a Trillion Thought-Controlled Serfs
Location: Earth, the Platinum Planet

A spaceship has been stolen by an escaped Treen. An interception squadron catch him and force him to turn back to Earth, but he has no intention of coming quietly. He crashes into one of the hangars on purpose, just to kill a few men. Dan tries to use the

Zyl ship *Zybalt* to help put out the fire, but an explosion in the hangar catches him and sends the *Zybalt* hurtling out of control into space.

As Dan and Digby try to repair the ship, they are knocked out by escaping Coma-Gas from the hibernation cabinets. When they awake the tank is empty and they realise they must have been asleep for years, travelling at full speed. They come upon a green planet unknown to them, and then they see another spaceship, which they follow until it lands on a platinum planet, or rather a planet covered by a platinum roof.

They manage to enter this 'building', but the inhabitants ignore them until Digby knocks one of their helmets off. They are captured and wake up wearing hypno-helmets, which force them to follow commands until they take them off. Because they refuse to follow the rules, they are ejected from the planet on to the green planet they saw earlier. They meet other refugees and discover that they are all meant to colonise the planet to make it habitable for the Platinums, after which they will be killed.

The inhabitants, led by Zeb, are not prepared to die; they have intercepted a ship from the Platinum Planet and plan to go there to get their own ships back. Dan and Digby volunteer to join in. The plan succeeds, they get back the *Zybalt* and make their escape, but are pursued. They could get away but choose to stay and help their friends in a dogfight. Zeb is fine: he has a ray which blows the fuses on the hypno-helmets. Dan determines to get that ray on to the planet to free all the serfs from Astorat's rule.

Zeb destroys the transmitter masts, and so the only thing left is to dethrone Astorat, which they manage without too much trouble. The boys head for home, having made another friend for life.

✳ 'The Earth Stealers'

2 December 1961 (Vol. 12, no. 48) to 3 March 1962 (Vol. 13, no. 9)

Main characters: Dan, Digby, Lex
Villain: Malvol
Location: Earth

Earth is deserted. Dan and Digby finally find some signs of life at 'Earth Reclamation Ltd', where one S. Malvol explains that the people of the Earth were evacuated when the ice-caps melted and a plague threatened humanity. Malvol has the contract to get Earth back into habitable shape. He gives them shelter and asks them to take the inoculation against the plague. Dan stops Dig taking it as he believes it is poison.

They decide to scarper and head for Mars in *Zybalt* to see if the Earth Government really is there. Malvol radios ahead to say there is an unauthorised flight on the way and an interceptor makes its way towards them and fires on them. They survive the attack but are unconscious and are picked up by the chaps from Space Fleet and taken to meet Controller Burke, who tells them Sir Hubert went on a deep-space trip just after they disappeared. He tells them he is not sure of Malvol but the government trust him. He leaves a ship for them to steal and head back to Earth, to get some evidence against Malvol.

They find Lex and discover that Malvol is controlling people with a mind drug; he plans to do the same to Dan, but Dan and Lex switch it for a saline solution. Dan and other pilots are sent to bomb Mars; they pretend to be obeying, then turn and take control, overpowering Malvol and foiling his plot.

✳ 'Operation Earthsaver'

10 March 1962 (Vol. 13, no. 10) to 9 June 1962 (Vol. 13, no. 23)

Main characters: Dan, Digby, Prof. Grainger
Villains: the Plants
Location: Earth

Plant life on Earth begins to grow out of control. Professor Grainger thinks it is due to some rays from outer space, but it's Earth's own Cosmic Ray research satellite. Dan, Digby and the professor set off to find and destroy it, and discover it is being used to relay a signal from deep space.

Back on Earth, the insects have begun to grow into massive beasts. An alien ship arrives and starts sucking up all the overgrown plant life, along with Digby, Dan and the professor. Inside the ship, they accidentally trip a switch, which starts the ship dumping its load. The spaceship then sets off and stops at a planet with rows and rows of enormous plants. The planet is ruled by plants, who send spaceships all over the galaxy to source fertiliser. On the planet they find the transmitter that is sending the signal to Earth. They destroy it, then make their way home aboard one of the harvest ships.

✳ 'The Evil One'

16 June 1962 (Vol. 13, no. 24) to 11 August 1962 (Vol. 13, no. 32)

Main characters: Dan, Digby, Charlie Barker, the Galactics
Villain: Professor van Malus
Location: Earth

Space Fleet Base on Moon Six of Jupiter is attacked and all are killed; their distress signal reached Earth too late. Dan and Digby go to investigate. As they reach the moon they see other ships approaching it, which are fired on. They receive a message from the head of the Galactics telling them that a malevolent creature they call 'the Evil One' is on the loose and heading for Earth. The Galactics are hunting it and will stop at nothing to find it, leaving destruction in their wake.

On a short leave during the crisis, Digby finds the creature, a fifteen-foot giant, by chance at his friend Charlie Barker's fun fair in Blackpool; but they are captured and used as bait to lure Dan to swap himself for them as a hostage.

As Dan becomes the Evil One's prisoner the Galactic force in search of the giant arrive, and launch a massive attack. Dan is determined that the giant has to die, even if it means his own death, but the giant escapes and carries on the fight.

Dan meanwhile discovers the giant's secret. He is being controlled by Professor van Malus, who escaped Earth many years ago, just before being tried for cruelty connected with evil experiments. Malus uses Dan as a decoy to pull the Galactic search away from himself, but he is trapped and killed as his HQ collapses on top of him. And so ends Digby's holiday.

✳

✳ 'Operation Fireball'

18 August 1962 (Vol. 13, no. 33) to 20 October 1962 (Vol. 13, no. 42)

Main characters: Dan, Digby
Villain: Mine Manager Cragg
Location: Earth, Mars

While chaperoning a routine freighter flight back from Mars, Dan and Digby watch in horror as it explodes and plummets to Earth. It lands in the sea, but rather than sinking it creates a massive fireball, which starts moving randomly around the planet, causing chaos, death and destruction wherever it goes.

They head off to Mars to find out the cause, and meet a mine manager, Cragg, who has come across some Martians who have found the secret to creating gold. Unfortunately the process is highly unstable and it is these raw materials, which Cragg put on the freighter, that are now causing the problem on Earth.

As they investigate further they find another material that counteracts the volatility of the fireball maker. Cragg is killed in the making of this discovery. With great care, Dan and Digby manage to take some of this material back to Earth and use it to neutralise the fireball.

✳ 'The Web of Fear'

27 October 1962 (Vol. 13, no. 43) to 29 December 1962 (Vol. 13, no. 52)

Main characters: Dan, Digby, Young
Villains: the Spiders
Location: Earth

Cadet Young, a pilot protégé of Dan's, crashes on his big test flight. He escapes but seems changed. As they rescue him a huge white cloud falls near by and kills everything it lands on before disappearing. A seemingly hypnotised Young gives a terrible warning that more such 'webs' will come.

Dan and Digby are sent to find the source. Dan decides Young should come along. The cadet takes the controls in a trance and flies to the moon. Once there he runs to a strange catacombed area, also covered with the webs. The crew decide to return to Earth, not noticing that huge spiders are hiding in the spaceship.

Back on Earth, the webs are dropping from the sky at an increasing rate and spawning more of the terrifying spiders. The whole planet is having similar outbreaks, but the armies of the world are winning the battle. Young comes out of his trance and warns them that the comet passing by in a few days must be destroyed or things will get worse.

The powers that be are not prepared to heed his warning as they are satisfied that the spiders have been brought under control. Peace reigns as the comet approaches and passes, but an hour after Earth has gone through its tail more webs begin to fall, and more spiders are hatched.

Ignoring orders, Dan and Digby, with Young in tow, decide to destroy the comet themselves. Close to they can see that it is a large incubator for the deadly arachnids. They get near enough to place explosives and, with Young's help, destroy the comet and save Earth.

✳ 'Operation Dark Star'

5 January 1963 (Vol. 14, no. 1) to 2 March 1963 (Vol. 14, no. 9)

Main characters: Dan, Digby, Egon
Villain: Naz
Location: Earth, an unnamed planet

Professor Egon has discovered the nearest star to Earth, and it has a planet in its orbit. Dan and Digby are to explore the planet, but Captain Egon, the professor's son, feels that he should be the first to make footfall on it. He causes Dan to have an accident and thus takes his place alongside Digby, with Dan to follow a fortnight later when his injury is healed.

Things go badly when Egon ignores Digby's advice and lands in a bad spot. Nothing has been heard from them by the time Dan and his crew arrive. They find a city, and it becomes clear that the scarcest commodity on this planet is water. They give the natives some in exchange for help in finding Digby and Egon.

There are two distinct groups on the planet, the ones Dan has bumped into, who work together to extract water where they can, and another, ruled by Naz, who use slaves to this job and have captured Digby and Egon.

Dan manages to free Digby and Egon, but Naz has hidden in their ship. When a Mexican stand-off ensues, Egon sacrifices himself so that the others can escape.

✳ 'Operation Time Trap'

9 March 1963 (Vol. 14, no. 10) to 28 September 1963 (Vol. 14, no. 38)

Main characters: Dan, Digby, Col. Banger, 'Nutter' Cobb, Major Spence
Villain: Xel
Location: Meit

Dan and Digby are assigned the honour of taking the *Tempus Frangit* on its maiden test flight. The translation of this Latin name is 'time breaks apart'. They are accompanied by the rather pernickety Major Spence and the gadget wizard Nutter Cobb.

The first 'time-jump' lands them in an empty blackness. The ship won't go back, and eventually they find a solar system with two suns and land on the nearest planet, Meit. It is mainly water, with floating swamps as the only land.

They are met by locals who look primitive but have advanced technology, including a translation machine that allows them to communicate, given to them by a previous visitor. Before long this visitor arrives. He is Xel, from the Svalokin Empire of Stoll, and demands passage for his chamberlain, Zym, and himself on the *Tempus Frangit*. This means Dan will have to leave two crew behind.

Noli, assistant to the village wise man, offers to help Dan and co. get away from the planet using knowledge only he and the old-timer have. Unfortunately the translators that Xel gave the villagers are also transmitters, so he knows exactly what Dan is planning. Noli wants a chronometer in return for his help, but the ship needs it to work. He tells them of a legend which is the key to their escape, but before he can divulge it Xel turns off the translating machine: he has hold of the wise man and can get the information from him.

Xel's men try to force their way on to the *Tempus* but the floating swamp on which it is sitting is hit by a wave. The motion, bizarrely, causes them severe seasickness and they retreat, but the ship is in danger of sinking. While this battle is going on Cobb has found a way to turn the translator back on and got the secret for their escape out of Noli. They just need to get to magnetic north at a specific time. Xel hears this at the same time as Dan, thanks to the bugging device hidden in the translator. Zyl sends Zym to trick his way on to the ship. Zym, terrified of Xel's wrath, is unsure whether to follow the plan or surrender to Dan. He goes along with the plan, keeping his options open, and explains how they can escape the magnetic pull of the planet.

The crew follow Zym's plan and prepare to leave, but Xel gets on to the ship unseen. He believes Zym has betrayed him and so kills him, then turns his gun on Dan. Digby manages to save him and they exit the ship, only to be captured by the Meitians. They persuade the Meitians that Xel is their common enemy and together they get Xel and his Stollites off the ship. They chase them back to their ship in the hope of defeating Xel and saving the wise elder, who is held captive.

On Xel's ship they accidentally stop the supply of drugs entering the food, thus loosening Xel's grip over his troops. The troops rebel and chase Xel, giving Dan and Digby the chance to look for the wise old man. The rebels set the ship on fire and Dan, Dig and the old guy just manage to escape, chased by Xel, who is desperate for revenge.

They make it back to *Tempus Frangit* and manage to get her moving. Unknown to them, as they try to get clear of the planet there is a stowaway on board. Can they pull out of the planet's gravity?

✳ 'The Wandering World'

5 October 1963 (Vol. 14, no. 39) to 28 March 1964 (Vol. 15, no. 13)

Main characters: Dan, Digby, Col. Banger, 'Nutter' Cobb, Major Spence
Villains: Xel, the Mekon
Location: Space

The *Tempus Frangit* escapes from Meit. They set the dials for Earth, but the calculations are off because they have a stowaway, Xel, who changes the weight. They therefore arrive millions of light years from Earth, with no fuel to reach it.

Xel is angered by their ineptitude, but they are all trapped and so they search the skies for a solution. In the distance they see a light approaching; it's a spaceship of sorts. It looks like a collection of bubbles.

Xel storms off to take it over, and Dan and Digby follow. Once on board they find their old enemy the Mekon. The ship turns out to be the last refuge of a race called Nav who have been in search of a new planet since their own was destroyed. They are helping the Mekon in return for his promise to give them part of Earth.

Both the Mekon and Xel make various attempts to kill Dan and co. Everyone wants the *Tempus* to get to Earth, but the Mekon is the only one with fuel.

A Nav overhears the Mekon telling Xel he will ditch them when he leaves, so they offer to help Dan. Xel gets hold of the Mekon's ship, but the green one has it on remote control, brings it back and almost burns Xel to death with the onboard security. Dan manages to get the Mekon off his saucer and into *Tempus*, and starts to head for home. The Mekon's spare fuel is ejected from the Nav ship and collected for the *Tempus*.

With control of both ships, and the Mekon and Xel locked up, Dan and the crew head gratefully for home.

✳ 'The Big City Caper'

---

5 April 1964 (Vol. 15, no. 14) to 30 May 1964 (Vol. 15, no. 22)

Main characters: Dan, Digby, Dicky Bird
Villain: Xel
Location: Earth

Following straight on from 'The Wandering World', Dan and Digby bring Xel and the Mekon back to Earth. The Mekon goes into a top-security prison to await trial, while Xel goes into a low-security hospital for treatment of his burns.

Xel escapes and uses the boredom of Earth's teenagers to cause havoc in London. With the help of Dickie Bird, he rounds up enough teens to commandeer the Post Office Tower and tries to take over London. One of the teens is Dan Dare's nephew, Nigel Dare.

The young people quickly get bored with being bossed about, and without their help he is quickly overpowered. Dan, realising the powder keg that is a teen with time on his hands, decides to set up a colony on a far-off planet where they can learn life skills.

✳ 'All Treens Must Die'

6 June 1964 (Vol. 15, no. 23) to 17 October 1964 (Vol. 15, no. 42)

Main characters: Dan, Digby, Sondar, Cobb, Banger
Villains: the Mekon, the Last Three
Location: Earth, Venus

This story follows on from 'The Big City Caper'. The Mekon escapes during his trial, thanks to help from some loyal Treens who are under the command of the Last Three. He uses a mind-altering drug to trick Banger and Cobb into taking him back to Venus.

On Venus, the Last Three have begun to create a new breed of red Treens. They are to replace the current green Treens, who have too often failed, and so like a faulty machine must be destroyed.

Dan and Digby follow the Mekon to Venus and find his secret bolthole, where the new Treens are being held in readiness and a vast armoury of machines is being built. The Mekon sets about his plan to kill all the current Treens by first hypnotising Sondar's Treens to commit suicide while his own Treens also kill any they come across.

Dan realises that his only chance is to find the Last Three and attack them in the hope that this will draw the Mekon out. While Digby helps Sondar defend Mekonta, Dan and Cobb head off to the Flame Lands to find the hiding place.

Once there they are separated and Dan is confronted by each of the Last Three in turn. Meanwhile Cobb, using his special tinkering skills, sends a message to the Mekon that the Last Three need his help.

Dan looks like he has had it when one of the Last Three passes him on for neurological testing and then death, but he manages to escape and kills one of the Last Three, snapping his neck. He goes after the next one, but the Mekon beats him to it. Disappointed that his most trusted advisers have let him down, the Mekon kills the remaining two. He is about to kill Dan when Digby blasts through the roof of the cavern and sends an avalanche of rocks crashing on to the Mekon. He falls into the murky depths, surely to his death.

Dan and Digby hope this at last will usher in a new era of peace on Venus and Earth.

✳ 'The Mushroom'

24 October 1964 (Vol. 15, no. 43) to 6 February 1965 (Vol. 16, no. 6)

Main characters: Dan, Digby, Hank, Banger
Villain: the Mekon
Location: Earth

Dan and Digby are on a routine patrol when they see something heading for Earth. Dan knows it can't be a meteorite as its tail is alight before it hits Earth's atmosphere. They report it, but nothing has shown up on Earth radars.

Hank Hogan, on holiday in London, stumbles across some suspicious Treens and is thrown out of the building they occupy. All Treens are on Earth under licence to behave themselves, so he reports it.

The two incidents are linked when Dan and Hank meet up and the Texan explains that he saw the Treens working on some kind of metallic mushroom. (During this meeting Hank also tells Dan that Prof. Peabody is now Mrs Jack Gurk.) This mushroom has grown from the seed that Dan and Digby saw heading for Earth. The next morning their fears are realised when the mushroom bursts through the ground in central London. It is being controlled from orbit and Dan and Digby are sent to trace the source while various attempts to destroy it are made, and fail.

The source is a satellite, in which sits the Mekon. He survived their last encounter and is now using this mushroom to blackmail the UN into giving him back control of Venus. He broadcasts to Londoners that they will all die unless the government gives in to his demands.

Dan and Digby get access to the Mekon's satellite, but he captures and paralyses them. He keeps them alive to watch his dastardly plan unfold.

Panic sets in as the mushroom begins to destroy London with rockets and death rays. The Mekon sends similar seeds to all the major capitals, while Londoners protest and plead with the government to give in.

Having tried ground and air attacks to destroy the mushroom, Colonel Banger comes up with the last resort. He arranges for the London Underground transport system to be packed with high explosives. This succeeds and the mushroom bursts into flames.

The Mekon's satellite is still sending intense signals to the mushroom, and as these are not being received the systems on the satellite overheat and are set to explode. All the Treens get into escape modules while Dan and Digby battle with the Mekon. They think they have him, but can't see because of the flames. They manage to get out of the satellite just before it destroys itself. In the distance they see a green object arcing away into space. The Mekon must have escaped, but at least Earth and Venus are safe. For now.

✳ 'The Moonsleepers'

13 February 1965 (Vol. 16, no. 7) to 17 July 1965 (Vol. 16, no. 29)

Main characters: Dan, Digby, Sir Hubert
Villains: Xel, the Mekon
Location: Earth, Triton

Having declined the offer to live peacefully on Earth, Xel is imprisoned alone in a floating space prison. It has enough food for two years, and he is to receive more supplies every eleven months.

Sir Hubert Guest is on his way back from Venus when his craft disappears. Dan and Digby investigate and find all the Therons aboard dead and Sir Hubert gone.

In Xel's satellite cell, the Mekon makes a bargain. He gives Xel a spaceship and Sir Hubert; in return Xel will help the Mekon regain his rightful place as ruler of Venus. Xel uses his mind control to make Sir Hubert tell him where he can find an army to use in his quest to take over Earth. While this attack is going on, the Mekon will attack Venus, thus splitting the universe's defence forces and making victory certain.

Xel takes Sir Hubert to Triton, Neptune's largest moon,

where there lives a lazy people, served by computers which are now in disrepair, making them ripe for Xel's type of leadership. Xel shoots Sir Hubert in the back and heads off to conquer these indolent folk.

Sir Hubert survives, and manages to leave in Xel's spaceship's escape capsule on a course for Earth. He knows the plan and must warn Space Fleet. Xel is unconcerned, as he does not believe this journey can be made in such a craft. He continues to build his forces.

Having been declared missing in action, Sir Hubert arrives back on Earth against all odds, and gives the warning. Dan and Digby set off for Triton in *Anastasia*. Once there they see that Xel is almost ready for the attack, but he steals *Anastasia* and they have to stow away in one of the attack ships in order to try to get home before him.

They just manage this. Space Fleet prepares for the defence and Dan believes that the Mekon will not attack Venus until Xel has defeated Earth, because he knows that the Therons will come to Earth's defence, leaving Venus unguarded. Dan therefore calls the Therons for assistance.

They arrive just in the nick of time, help Space Fleet overcome Xel's onslaught and have enough time to return home to pre-empt the Mekon's strike. Seeing his plan has been foiled, the Mekon disappears into the skies.

✳ 'The Singing Scourge'

24 July 1965 (Vol. 16, no. 30) to 5 February 1966 (Vol. 17, no. 6)

Main characters: Dan, Digby, Banger, Cobb, Professor Smith
Villains: Reshnek, Koob
Location: Lapri, Volk

Digby is delighted when a hiking holiday with Dan is interrupted by a call to return to Space Fleet HQ. Professor John F. Smith has discovered a sound wave being emitted in a far-off galaxy near the star Vega, which he believes could be the source of a new form of energy. In the *Tempus Frangit*, these three, plus Cobb and Banger, set off to find it.

Once they have made the 'time-jump', they see two planets so close to each other that their atmospheres are joined. They land on the most hospitable-looking one, Lapri, only to be surprised by the joyous welcome they receive. They are taken to the nearest city by the locals, the Trons, but then everyone is rounded up by fearsome four-armed nasties called Vendals.

One of the Trons explains how the Vendals appeared from the skies to ruin their peaceful rural existence. But the prophecy is that a second force will arrive to save them, hence the celebratory welcoming committee.

They are taken to a place of execution and a radiation weapon, the Singing Scourge, is directed at them by Reshnek, leader of the Vendals. Thanks to their space suits, the team survive and the Trons celebrate as the prophecy must surely come true. As punishment for not dying, the Vendals banish them to the Black Deserts of Volk, the other planet, where everything has died at the hands of the Singing Scourge. On Volk are many other exiles, both Tron and Vendal, who have fallen foul of Reshnek's rule.

They meet a Vendal called Koob, who discovered the Scourge, but was ill so he too was exiled. Koob offers to help them overcome the Vendal settlement to get power on Volk, and so, with an army of Trons, they attack. Dan's main aim, of course, is to secure the deadly Scourge.

They trick Reshnek into believing the Scourge no longer works by sending remote-controlled armoured vehicles to the defences. Reshnek abandons the city to head back to Lapri, but has the Scourge with him. Dan and the team follow; they know it still works and they need it for Earth. Reshnek does not realise that Koob has stowed away on his escape ship. Koob now uses the Scourge to kill everyone else on the ship, but realises too late that he cannot fly the ship alone, and it crashes into Lapri.

Dan arrives, and fights off the Vendals to secure the evil weapon. Once he has it, they head back to the *Tempus Frangit* and home.

*

✱ 'Give Me the Moon'

12 February 1966 (Vol. 17, no. 7) to 25 June 1966 (Vol. 17, no. 26)

Main characters: Dan, Digby, Banger, Cobb, Professor Smith
Villain: Benny Clark a.k.a. Laslo Romanov
Location: Earth, Moon

Arriving home two and half years after setting off for Vega, Dan is warned of certain changes. One of the main ones is the new automated freighter system between Earth and Venus.

Within a few days of his return this remote-controlled shuttle system is under attack from a terrorist organisation called FIST. They demand the Moon, otherwise they will continue to stop food being transported back from Venus.

Space Fleet does not deal with terrorists, but they cannot find out anything about this group, who seem to have an ear on everything Space Fleet does. The only clue is that their hardware seems to come from M Industries, the company that used to be run by the now-dead Laslo Romanov. Space Fleet are stumped, until John F. Smith tracks some of the signals to an unknown satellite in space. This first vital clue leads them back to Benny Clark, an innocuous-seeming commissionaire at HQ.

It turns out that Clark is actually Romanov, and his job at HQ has given him access to every effort that has been made to stop him. When he is finally discovered he destroys his evil empire and kills himself.

✱ 'The Menace from Jupiter'

2 July 1966 (Vol. 17, no. 27) to 7 January 1967 (Vol. 18, no. 1)

Main characters: Dan, Digby, Bro
Villains: the Pittars
Location: Earth, Jupiter

Dan is sent to investigate an unidentified spaceship which has crashed into the Atlantic. Aboard, he finds a small alien called Bro who has come from Jupiter to seek help; his people, the Verans, are under threat from a giant race called the Pittars. He explains that once Jupiter is conquered, Earth will be next.

Dan and Digby go with him to Jupiter but Bro's own people are not sure of Dan and Digby, even of Bro, and hand them over to the Pittars in the hope of reward or peace. They are killed for their trouble.

Dan and Digby are put in an arena to save Bro's life, as amusement for the Pittar overlord. They show great courage but during the trial the overlord starts sneezing. Having never suffered disease before, he cannot cope and runs amok to such an extent that his underlings feel they have to kill him. Afraid for their own lives at the threat of a common cold, they depart Jupiter, leaving the Verans in peace, and Dan as the saviour of yet another race, although here it was Digby's cold that did the trick.

Back on Earth, Dan is promoted to controller of the fleet. His first task is to chronicle his adventures for the benefit of Space Fleet cadets.

✳ 'Underwater Attack'

30 December 1967 (Vol. 18, no. 52) to 20 January 1968 (Vol. 19, no. 3)

Main characters: Dan, Digby
Villain: none
Location: Earth

On a snorkelling holiday in Greece, Dan and Digby spot what look like some strange aliens behaving suspiciously. Fearless as ever, they abandon their holiday to investigate, only to discover that they are not aliens but naval personnel involved with top-secret experiments.

BIBLIOGRAPHY

'Dan Dare Got There First!': catalogue for fiftieth anniversary exhibition at Croydon Clocktower 2000.

Odyssey, The Authorised Biography of Arthur C. Clarke, Neil McAleer, Victor Gollancz 1992

True to Type, Ruari McLean, Werner Shaw 2000

Living with Eagles, Sally Morris and Jan Hallwood, Lutterworth Press 1998

The Man Who Drew Tomorrow, Alastair Crompton, Who Dares 1985

Before I Die Again, Chad Varah, Constable Robinson 1992

The Dan Dare Dossier, Norman Wright, Hawk Books 1990

The Best of Eagle, Marcus Morris, Michael Joseph and Ebury Press 1977

'Interview with Frank Hampson by Penny Clarke', Learning Resources, Brighton Polytechnic 1978

Dan Dare Pilot of the Future [Adventure Reprints] Titan Books

Spaceship Away, Rod Barzilay 2003–2010

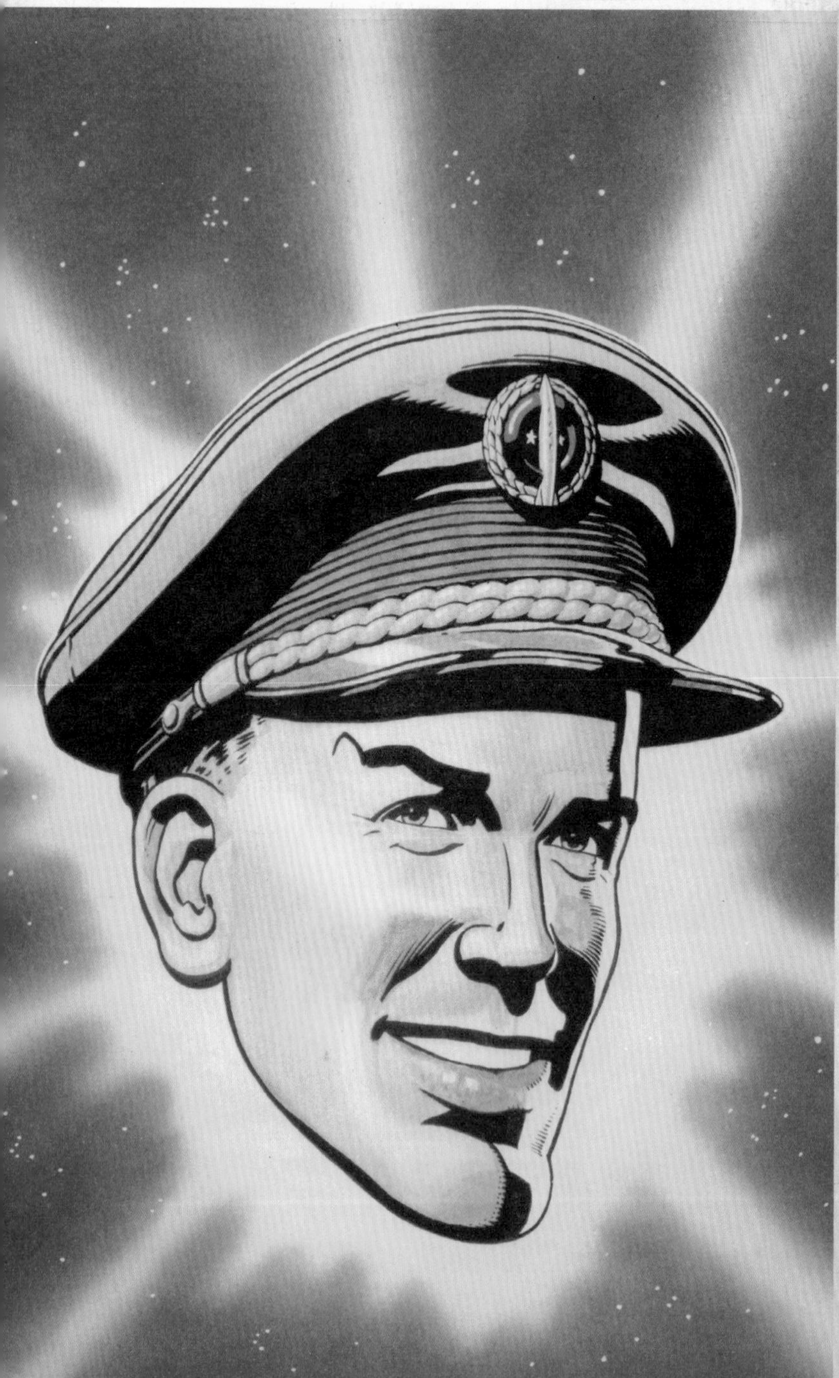

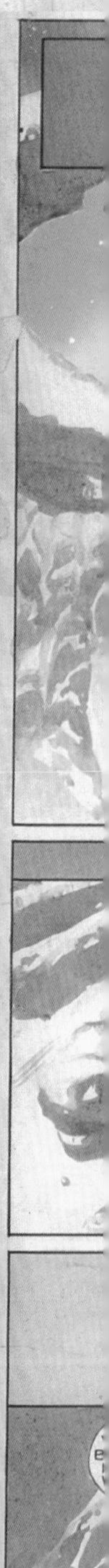